Falkland Islands Review

Report of a Committee
of
Privy Counsellors

Chairman:
The Rt Hon The Lord Franks, OM, GCMG, KCB, CBE

Presented to Parliament by the Prime Minister
by Command of Her Majesty
January 1983

LONDON
HER MAJESTY'S STATIONERY OFFICE
£6·10 net

Cmnd. 8787

MEMBERS OF THE COMMITTEE

The Rt. Hon. The Lord Franks, O M, G C M G, K C B, C B E (Chairman)

The Rt. Hon. The Lord Barber, T D

The Rt. Hon. The Lord Lever of Manchester

The Rt. Hon. Sir Patrick Nairne, G C B, M C

The Rt. Hon. Merlyn Rees, M P

The Rt. Hon. The Lord Watkinson, C H

TABLE OF CONTENTS

iii

Note : the estimated cost of preparing the report, including staff costs is £81,800.

INTRODUCTION

On 6 July 1982, in a Written Answer to a Parliamentary Question,[1] the Prime Minister announced that, following consultation with the Leader of the Opposition and leaders of other Opposition parties, the Government had decided to appoint a committee of Privy Counsellors, under the chairmanship of Lord Franks, with the following terms of reference:

" To review the way in which the responsibilities of Government in relation to the Falkland Islands and their Dependencies were discharged in the period leading up to the Argentine invasion of the Falkland Islands on 2 April 1982, taking account of all such factors in previous years as are relevant; and to report ".

In answer to a separate Question on the same day,[2] the Prime Minister announced the names of the other members of the Committee.

2. After a debate, the House of Commons resolved on 8 July to approve the Government's decision to set up a Falkland Islands review.[3]

3. We met for the first time on 26 July and held 42 meetings, on all but two occasions for the whole of the day.

4. In her opening speech in the debate on 8 July, the Prime Minister made it clear that the Committee should have access to all relevant papers and persons. All the Government Departments concerned provided us with papers relevant to our review. We subsequently asked for, and received, personal and formal written assurances from the Secretary of the Cabinet, the Permanent Under-Secretaries of State at the Foreign and Commonwealth Office and the Ministry of Defence, and the Permanent Secretary to the Treasury that to the best of their knowledge and belief all the papers in their Departments relevant to our terms of reference had been brought to our attention.

5. We were provided with the following documents:

   (i) folders of all the relevant papers that the Prime Minister personally saw from the time the present Government took office to 2 April 1982;

   (ii) all relevant Cabinet and Cabinet Committee[4] papers and minutes of meetings from 1965 onwards;

   (iii) detailed memoranda prepared by the Foreign and Commonwealth Office Research Department on the history of the dispute from 1965, various other papers and, for the period from the beginning of 1976 onwards, a comprehensive set of documents;

   (iv) a comprehensive set of Ministry of Defence documents covering the period from 1965;

   (v) comprehensive sets of Treasury, Department of Energy, Home Office and Department of Trade documents;

---

[1] *Official Report*, House of Commons, 6 July 1982, Written Answers, Col. 51.
[2] *Official Report*, House of Commons, 6 July 1982, Written Answers, Col. 52.
[3] *Official Report*, House of Commons, 8 July 1982, Cols. 469–508.
[4] Annex B contains a brief account of relevant aspects of the machinery of Government including the Defence and Oversea Policy Committee and the Joint Intelligence Organisation.

1

(vi) every report from the intelligence agencies relating to the Falkland Islands from the beginning of 1981 until 2 April 1982, and a large number of reports from previous years, including all those circulated in 1976 and 1977; and

(vii) every assessment on Argentina and the Falkland Islands made by the Joint Intelligence Organisation([1]) since 1965, together with any relevant minutes of meetings.

6. In addition, at our request, all relevant Foreign and Commonwealth Office and Ministry of Defence files for the first three months of 1982 were placed in our offices for the duration of our review. We also asked for, and received, papers on a number of specific aspects of our remit, and we were provided with reports from the intelligence agencies received after 2 April that threw light on the events leading up to the invasion. Any files for previous years were freely available for our inspection, and we took advantage of this facility to obtain a number of documents that we thought relevant. We received every assistance from all Departments in our review, and all our requests for additional papers and information were met.

7. At our first meeting we decided on a programme of work with the aim of submitting a report within six months. We decided that, given the nature of our task, it would not be satisfactory to rely on summaries, however accurate and comprehensive, of the papers provided, and we set aside a large part of August and September to enable each member of the Committee to read individually the documents available to us.

8. On 26 July we issued a press statement in the following terms:

" The Committee held its first meeting today (26 July 1982). It has a further programme of meetings. It does not intend at this stage to issue any further statements about the progress of its work.

" The Committee will in due course be taking oral evidence at its own invitation. But it also invites anyone who has information which might assist it in considering its remit to submit evidence in writing by 30 August 1982 to the Secretary, Falkland Islands Review Committee, Old Admiralty Building, Whitehall, London, SW1."

This statement was repeated by the Prime Minister in reply to a Parliamentary Question on 20 July.([2]) We received written submissions in response to this invitation from a number of individuals and organisations, whose names are listed in Annex C. We have studied them all with care and we are grateful to all those who wrote to us. We have also studied a number of books and articles, mainly written after the invasion, that bear on our terms of reference.

9. On our instructions, the Secretary wrote to the editors of all the national newspapers, to the Secretary of the Newspaper Society, who passed on our request to the editors of provincial newspapers, and to several periodicals asking whether they had any specific information in the first three months of the year which indicated the possibility of Argentine action against the Falkland Islands. Those who sent replies other than acknowledgements are listed in Annex D.

([1]) Annex B contains a brief account of relevant aspects of the machinery of Government, including the Defence and Oversea Policy Committee and the Joint Intelligence Organisation.

([2]) *Official Report*, House of Commons, 29 July 1982, Written Answers, Col. 617.

10. We decided that, in addition to reading the documents, we should talk to those principally involved, both Ministers and officials, in the development of the present Government's Falkland Islands policy; to some Ministers of previous administrations, including all the former Prime Ministers for the period covered by our review; to persons with a special knowledge of and interest in the area; to representatives of the broadcasting media; and to some journalists. We devoted the period from the end of September to the beginning of November largely to taking oral evidence. We held 39 sessions of oral evidence. Those who gave oral evidence to us are listed in Annex E.

11. We wish to express our gratitude to those who have formed the staff of the Committee. In particular, we record our high appreciation of the services of our Secretary, Mr. Anthony Rawsthorne, who has carried out his duties with resourcefulness, skill and judgment. He has been ably assisted in all his duties by our Assistant Secretary, Mr. Peter Moulson. We also wish to thank Mr. David Smith, who has taken responsibility for the many and varied arrangements our work has entailed, and our Personal Secretary, Miss Joan Frank, who, in addition to her other duties, typed drafts with speed and accuracy. The whole staff rapidly acquired accurate knowledge of the subject-matter of our terms of reference and made a complex programme of oral hearings and private meetings easy to fulfil. We are glad to acknowledge our indebtedness to them all.

12. The main body of our report is in four sections. Chapter 1 contains an account of the dispute between the United Kingdom and Argentina from 1965 to 1979; Chapter 2 describes in more detail the sequence of events and the development of policy since the present Government took office; Chapter 3 contains a detailed account of events from the landing of a party of Argentine scrap merchants on South Georgia on 19 March 1982 to the invasion of the Falkland Islands on 2 April; and Chapter 4 sets out the judgments we have reached on the basis of our examination of the narrative of events set out in the preceding chapters. Annex A contains a refutation of some of the more important assertions and allegations that have been made in the press and elsewhere.

13. In our review we have taken particular care to avoid the exercise of hindsight in reaching judgments on the development of policy and on the actions of Ministers and officials. We have sought to judge on each important issue whether the views expressed and the action taken by those concerned were reasonable in the light of the information available to them and the circumstances prevailing at the time, and not to substitute our judgment of what we might have done in those circumstances.

14. We have also borne in mind that our task required us to focus exclusively on the Government's responsibilities for the Falkland Islands and the Dependencies, whereas those concerned, both Ministers and officials, had to deal with many other major and pressing preoccupations.

3

B*

Chapter 1

AN ACCOUNT OF THE DISPUTE FROM 1965 TO 1979

The starting point of the review

15. Our terms of reference required us to review the way in which the responsibilities of Government were discharged " in the period leading up to the Argentine invasion of the Falkland Islands on 2 April 1982, taking account of all such factors in previous years as are relevant ". We examine the events of that period in Chapters 2 and 3 of the Report.

16. In order to identify relevant factors in previous years we examined the history of the dispute between the United Kingdom and Argentina from 1965. 1965 provides a starting point, since it was then that the issue was first brought formally to international attention. This Chapter summarises the principal events from 1965 until the present Government took office in 1979. We have not attempted to write a comprehensive history of the dispute, but to present an account of it as the background against which more recent events should be seen. We describe the events of 1976 and 1977 in more detail than those of other years, since before 1981 this was a time of particular tension between Argentina and the United Kingdom, and parallels have been drawn between these two years and 1982.

1965–1975

The involvement of the United Nations

17. In 1963 and 1964 there was a resurgence of Argentine interest in the Falklands and a campaign was mounted in Argentina in support of its claim to the Islands. In addition to various official measures, such as the inauguration of a ' Malvinas Day ', an Argentine civilian landed a light aircraft at Port Stanley in September 1964, planted an Argentine flag in the ground, handed a proclamation to a bystander, and took off again. The Argentine Government publicly dissociated themselves from this incident.

18. In 1964 the Argentine Government raised the matter in the United Nations, in a sub-committee of the Special Committee on the situation with regard to the implementation of the Declaration of the Granting of Independence to Colonial Countries and Peoples (The Committee of 24). In reply the British Representative on The Committee of 24 declared that the British Government held that the question of sovereignty over the Islands was not negotiable, but they were willing to discuss the maintenance and development of peaceful relations between the United Kingdom and the Falkland Islands on the one hand and Argentina on the other. Following the Special Committee's report, a Resolution (No. 2065) was passed on 16 December 1965 at the General Assembly. It referred in its preamble to the " cherished aim of bringing to an end everywhere colonialism in all its forms, one of which covers the case of the Falkland Islands (Malvinas) "; invited the Governments of Argentina and of the United Kingdom to proceed without delay with negotiations with a view to finding a peaceful solution to the problem " bearing in mind the provisions and objectives of the Charter of the United Nations and of Resolution 154(XV) [on colonialism] and in the interests of the population of the Falkland Islands (Malvinas) "; and requested the two Governments to report to the Special Committee, and to the General Assembly at its next session.

Assessment of Argentine threat

19. In March 1965, the Joint Intelligence Committee[1] had re-assessed the external threat to the Falkland Islands and Dependencies. It considered that it was unlikely that the Argentine Government would launch an assault against the Islands, but that, if an unofficial party of raiders were able to obtain a footing on the Falklands, the attitude of the Argentine Government might change radically and rapidly under pressure of public opinion.

First diplomatic exchanges

20. The Argentine claim to the Islands was raised with the Foreign Secretary, Mr. Michael Stewart (as he then was), when he visited Buenos Aires in January 1966; and in July a preliminary meeting was held in London, at which the Argentine Ambassador submitted a note formally claiming the " restitution " of the Falkland Islands to Argentina. The British delegation rejected the implication that Britain's occupation of the Islands was illegal, but there was agreement that there should be detailed examination at a later date of ways of decreasing friction and of limiting the scale of the dispute.

' Operation Condor '

21. In September 1966 a further unofficial incident, known as ' Operation Condor ', took place. An armed group of 20 young Argentines hijacked an Argentine Airlines DC4 and forced it to go to the Falklands, where it landed on the race-course at Port Stanley. As in 1964, the Argentine Government publicly dissociated themselves from the incident, but there were demonstrations throughout Argentina in support of the Argentine claim to the Islands, and shots were fired at the British Embassy in Buenos Aires while the Duke of Edinburgh was on an official visit there. In the light of the ' Condor ' incident, the Royal Marine detachment on the Islands, which had been established in 1965 but reduced to one officer and five men in 1966, was restored to platoon strength. Although consideration was subsequently given from time to time to its withdrawal, it was retained at that level thereafter.

The ' Memorandum of Understanding '

22. Further talks were held in November 1966, and in 1967. In a paper to the Defence and Oversea Policy Committee[2] in preparation for the talks in November 1966, the Foreign and Colonial Secretaries (Mr. George Brown and Mr. Fred Lee (as they then were)) pointed out that Argentina could easily occupy the Islands by force. At the talks the British side initially proposed a ' sovereignty freeze ' for a minimum of 30 years, to allow for normalisation of relations between the Islands and Argentina while each side's position on sovereignty was protected. At the end of this period the Islanders would be free to choose between British and Argentine rule. The Argentine Government rejected this proposal, and in March 1967 the British Government for the first time stated formally to Argentina that they would be prepared to cede sovereignty over the Islands under certain conditions,

---

[1] For a description of the role and composition of the Joint Intelligence Committee see Annex B.

[2] For a description of the composition and functions of the Defence and Oversea Policy Committee see Annex B. For the sake of brevity we refer to it as the Defence Committee.

5

provided that the wishes of the Islanders were respected. Negotiations at official level were directed to agreeing the text, *ad referendum* to Governments, of a 'Memorandum of Understanding'. Early in 1968 the Governor of the Falkland Islands showed the Islands' Executive Council in confidence the text of an early version of the Memorandum. On 27 February 1968 the unofficial members of the Council sent an open letter to all Members of Parliament stating that negotiations were proceeding between the British and Argentine Governments " which may result at any moment in the handing over of the Falkland Islands to the Argentines ".([1]) There were strong protests in Parliament and in the press, and the Foreign and Commonwealth Secretary, Mr. Stewart, and other Foreign Office Ministers made clear on several occasions that there would be no cession of sovereignty against the wishes of the Islanders.([2])

23. Agreement on the text of the Memorandum of Understanding was reached at official level in August 1968. On sovereignty the crucial passage was as follows:

" The Government of the United Kingdom as part of such a final settlement will recognise Argentina's sovereignty over the Islands from a date to be agreed. This date will be agreed as soon as possible after (i) the two governments have resolved the present divergence between them as to the criteria according to which the United Kingdom Government shall consider whether the interests of the Islanders would be secured by the safeguards and guarantees to be offered by the Argentine Government, and (ii) the Government of the United Kingdom are then satisfied that those interests are so secured."

24. Publication of the Memorandum was to be accompanied by a unilateral statement making it clear that the Government would be willing to proceed to a final settlement with Argentina that involved the transfer of sovereignty, but only if and when they were satisfied that the transfer of sovereignty, and the basis on which such a transfer should take place, were acceptable to the people of the Islands.

25. Lord Chalfont, Minister of State at the Foreign and Commonwealth Office, visited the Islands in November 1968 to explain the policy that the Government had been pursuing in their talks with the Argentine Government. On his return the Government made statements in both Houses of Parliament on 3 December 1968 about Lord Chalfont's visit.([3]) They received a critical reception and were widely reported in the press. In view of the Parliamentary and press reaction, the Government decided at a Cabinet meeting on 11 December not to continue to attempt to reach a settlement on the basis of the Memorandum of Understanding, since Argentina was not prepared to accept either that the Memorandum should include a statement that any transfer of sovereignty would be subject to the wishes of the Islanders; or that the unilateral statement, enshrining this safeguard, should

---

([1]) In March 1968 in response to these events the Falkland Islands Emergency Committee, an unofficial body, was formed to bring to notice in the United Kingdom the wishes of the Falkland Islanders regarding their future. In 1973 it was renamed the United Kingdom Falkland Islands Committee. Its membership includes Members of Parliament of the main political parties.

([2]) *Official Report*, House of Commons, 26 March 1968, Col. 1464; 28 March 1968, Col. 1871; and 1 April 1968, Col. 4.

([3]) *Official Report*, House of Commons, 3 December 1968, Cols. 1254–1268; House of Lords, 3 December 1968, Cols. 24–36.

be specifically linked to the Memorandum. It was recognised, however, that failure to reach an understanding with Argentina carried the risks of increased harassment of the Islanders and the possibility of an attack. The Government therefore decided to endeavour to continue negotiations with Argentina while making clear the British attitude on sovereignty. Mr. Stewart made a statement in Parliament later the same day, which announced the decision to continue negotiations and which confirmed that the British Government would continue to insist on the paramountcy of the Islanders' wishes.[1]

The Communications Agreements

26. In 1969 talks were resumed. They were continued, following the change of Government in June 1970, by Mr. Heath's administration, but sovereignty was not discussed. Progress was reported to Parliament annually.[2] The talks were concerned with improving communications between Argentina and the Islands and were held without prejudice to either side's position on sovereignty. (This was known as the ' sovereignty umbrella '.) In 1971 agreement was reached on a wide range of communications matters, of which the most important was the establishment of air and sea services between the Islands and Argentina, to be provided by Argentina and the United Kingdom respectively. Other matters covered in the Agreements were the provision by Argentina of a travel document (the ' white card '), which would guarantee freedom of movement within Argentina for residents of the Islands and serve as the only documentation necessary for Argentine residents travelling to the Islands; certain reciprocal exemptions from duties and taxes; exemption for residents of the Islands from any obligation to Argentine military service; the harmonisation of postal, telegraphic and telephone rates with the rates obtaining in the country of origin; provision of school places and scholarships in Argentina for children in the Islands; and the establishment of a special consultative committee in Buenos Aires, consisting of representatives of the Argentine Ministry of Foreign Affairs and the British Embassy, to deal with questions arising over the setting up and promotion of communications in both directions. The Agreements were set out in a joint statement signed by both Governments, the text of which was reported to the House of Commons in September 1971.[3]

27. Following the Agreements, the Argentine Government returned to the question of sovereignty, and in January 1972 called for a resumption of the talks held between 1966 and 1968. They said that they would accept further talks on communications only if the British Government accepted later discussions on sovereignty in London.

28. Nevertheless, in a separate agreement concluded in May 1972, the Argentine authorities undertook to build a temporary airstrip (which came into operation in November 1972) to enable land-based aircraft to replace the amphibian service that they had provided up to then.

---

[1] *Official Report*, House of Commons, 11 December 1968, Cols. 424–434.

[2] *Official Report*, House of Commons, 24 November 1969, Cols. 36–40.
   Official Report, House of Commons, 16 November 1970, Written Answers, Col. 309.
   Official Report, House of Commons, 21 June 1971, Written Answers, Col. 178.

[3] *Official Report*, House of Commons, 23 September 1971, Written Answers, Cols. 13–17.

Condominium

29. Further exchanges followed, in which the Argentine Government pressed strongly for renewed negotiations on sovereignty while the British Government sought to establish that the talks did not constitute negotiations on that issue. In the course of 1973, however, it became clear that an impasse had been reached. Argentina again took the issue to the United Nations, where the Special Committee adopted a resolution, which formed the basis of a further Resolution (3160(XXVIII)) passed by the General Assembly calling on both parties to accelerate negotiations towards a solution of the sovereignty issue. In January 1974 the Defence Committee agreed that, in view of the pressure in the United Nations to reach a settlement and the risks of economic and military action against the Islands, the likely attitude of the Islanders to the possibility of condominium as an alternative to a transfer of sovereignty should be discussed with the Governor of the Falkland Islands. The Governor and the British Ambassador in Buenos Aires advised that in their opinion the idea was worth pursuing. Before this could be done, the General Election of March 1974 led to a change of Government. A Labour Government took office, with Mr. Wilson (as he then was) as Prime Minister and Mr. Callaghan as Foreign and Commonwealth Secretary.

30. The new Government, having been presented with a range of options, decided in the Defence Committee to consult the Falkland Islands Executive Council on the possibility of initiating talks with Argentina on condominium. The Council indicated that it would raise no objection to talks on condominium going ahead, provided that there was no Islander participation initially. The subject of condominium was broached with the Argentine Government; but, in the face of the Islanders' continuing refusal to participate, it was decided that there would be no purpose in proceeding without them, and the Argentine Government were so informed in August 1974. Despite this setback, further commercial agreements were concluded in September 1974, the most important being one providing for *Yaciementos Petroliferos*, the Argentine State Oil Company, to supply certain petroleum products on the Islands at mainland prices.

Increased Argentine pressure

31. In December 1974 an Argentine newspaper, *Cronica*, mounted a press campaign advocating invasion of the Islands. The Argentine Government publicly dissociated themselves from it, their Minister for Foreign Affairs, Sr. Vignes, informing Congress that he preferred negotiation to invasion. Nevertheless, following remarks made by Sr. Vignes to the press in March 1975, a few days before the arrival of the new British Ambassador in Buenos Aires, the Ambassador was instructed to warn him that an attack on the Islands would meet with a military response. The British Ambassador delivered this warning to Sr. Vignes in April 1975, at his first meeting with him.

Intelligence assessments

32. Over the period from 1965 to 1975 assessments were made by the Joint Intelligence Committee, usually about once a year but more frequently at times of increased tension. In the earlier years the conclusions were, broadly speaking, that official military action against the Falkland Islands

and the Dependencies was unlikely, at least until diplomatic means of settling the dispute had been exhausted, but that there was a continuing risk of unofficial action. In the early 1970s, when the Communications Agreements had led to improved relations with Argentina, the assessments were that direct military action could be discounted and that even the risk of an 'adventurist' operation was very slight. Towards the end of 1973 it was thought that Argentine attitudes were hardening, and for the first time there were indications that the Argentine Government (of President Peron) might be preparing contingency plans for an occupation of the Islands. In 1974 the Joint Intelligence Committee assessed that 'adventurist' operations were still the main threat, but with less likelihood of the Argentine Government's discouraging them; official military action was thought unlikely, as long as Argentina believed that the British Government were prepared to negotiate on sovereignty, but it was not ruled out.

Increased tension 1975–1977

Economic development

33. The next British initiative was a proposal, approved by the Defence Committee in July 1975, for discussions of joint Anglo-Argentine development of the resources of the South-West Atlantic. In response to this proposal Sr. Vignes suggested linking such an initiative to the possibility of a transfer of sovereignty followed by simultaneous leaseback for a period of years, as a means of settling the dispute. He also proposed that Argentina should occupy the uninhabited islands of South Georgia and the South Sandwich Islands, and that the occupation should be accepted without condemnation by the British Government. Sr. Vignes was warned that any such unilateral action would be quite unacceptable. The Argentine Government rejected the Government's proposal for talks on economic co-operation, which they saw as excluding discussion of the sovereignty issue.

The Shackleton survey

34. As a result of growing concern about the decline of the Falkland Islands' economy and the Islands' loss of population, the Government commissioned a comprehensive, long-term economic survey, under the leadership of Lord Shackleton, of the possibilities for the development of the Falkland Islands and the Dependencies. The terms of reference for the survey were drawn up in consultation with the Falkland Islands Executive Council and were announced in October 1975. This provoked a very hostile reaction in Argentina. The Argentine Ministry of Foreign Affairs issued a *communiqué* stating that the survey was an unwelcome initiative, to which Argentina had not agreed. The survey went ahead and the Shackleton Report was published in May 1976 (see paragraph 58 for the Government's response to it).

Argentine action at the United Nations

35. On 8 December 1975 the Argentine Representative at the United Nations made a long speech on the dispute at a plenary session of the General Assembly, in which he said:

"We are prepared to continue our efforts, but the limits of our patience and tolerance should not be underestimated if we should have to face an obstinate and unjustified refusal to negotiate by the other party".

He concluded by saying:

"The Argentine Government reserves its position regarding the responsibility which rests with the British Government for the breaking-off of negotiations and will not fail to assert its rights in the form which it deems most appropriate."

Worsening diplomatic relations

36. On 2 January 1976 the Argentine Foreign Minister, then Sr. Arauz Castex, sent a reply to messages from Mr. Callaghan about the Shackleton survey. Sr. Arauz Castex described the arrival in the Islands of Lord Shackleton's team on the anniversary of their " illegal occupation " by Britain in 1833 as an " unfriendly and unthoughtful " coincidence; expressed the Argentine Government's understanding that the British Government had unilaterally broken off negotiations; and referred to the " decidedly negative implications " of the British Government's attitude, and to their exclusive responsibility for breaking off negotiations. In giving this message to the British Ambassador in Buenos Aires, Sr. Arauz Castex said that, if the British Government refused to resume negotiations, " we were rapidly moving towards a head-on collision . . . in the end he could only see one course open to Argentina irrespective of what Government might be in power . . . Fortified by the support of the entire Argentine nation as well as all the other nations of the world assembled in New York, his Government could accept no responsibility for such a disastrous outcome ". On the same day the Argentine Ministry of Foreign Affairs issued a press *communiqué* referring to the British Government's unilateral breaking off of negotiations and concluding:

"The people of the Republic should take note that its Government, together with the armed forces and the other institutional organisations which make up the Argentine State, share an unbreakable zeal for the defence of the dignity and rights of the nation, and that they will act without precipitation but with all the persistence, prudence and energy which may be necessary to achieve justice."

37. Mr. Callaghan sent a conciliatory reply to Sr. Arauz Castex on 12 January, in which he offered to send a senior official to hold confidential discussions. The Argentine reply on 13 January expressed regret at not finding in it any " positive elements " with regard to the reopening of negotiations on sovereignty, and took exception to Mr. Callaghan's reference to a " sterile " dispute. It was announced in a press *communiqué* the same day that the Argentine Government had decided not to send their Ambassador back to London and to " suggest " that the British Ambassador in Buenos Aires should be withdrawn.

38. There was hostile press comment in Argentina in the first weeks of 1976. The British Embassy in Buenos Aires reported that some newspapers had advocated invasion " in veiled terms ". Some of the popular newspapers, evidently briefed by the Argentine Ministry of Foreign Affairs, published reports in the middle of the month of a long meeting which the Argentine Foreign Minister had held to consider counter measures. Unspecified " firm " and " concrete " decisions were promised. But the British Embassy reported on 21 January that, while the Argentine popular press " had been waging their usual campaign over the Islands over the last couple of weeks ", there had been no repetition of the invasion campaign run by

Cronica the previous year. A further report a week later stated that the storm that had blown up at the beginning of the month had at last begun to abate; there were indications that the Argentine Government had not wished to allow the " anti-British bandwagon " to get out of control; there had been no threats or demonstrations against the Embassy.

39. Mr. Callaghan made a statement in the Commons on 14 January 1976(¹) in conciliatory terms concluding that " given goodwill on both sides, Britain and Argentina should be able to transform the area of dispute concerning sovereignty over the Islands into a factor making for co-operation between the two countries which would be consonant with the wishes and interests of the Falkland Islanders ".

Intelligence reports and assessments

40. In November 1975 the Joint Intelligence Committee had prepared a new assessment on the Falkland Islands. It concluded that a deliberately planned invasion of the Falkland Islands in the near future still seemed unlikely but could not be wholly excluded. It followed earlier assessments in judging that there was a greater possibility of some kind of ' adventurist ' operation, particularly if the Shackleton survey went ahead in the face of continued public Argentine opposition: this opposition might be expressed by a propaganda campaign and possibly some practical harassment of the Falkland Islanders; the suspension of the air service would be an easy measure for Argentina to take.

41. In a further assessment on 8 January 1976 the Joint Intelligence Committee concluded that Argentina was unlikely to launch a sudden invasion in the near future, but that the likelihood had increased of the Argentine Government's intensifying political pressures and taking specific measures, such as the recall of Ambassadors and the suspension of the air service. It concluded that physical aggression remained a remoter prospect, but certainly could not be excluded. On 22 January 1976 a further assessment was prepared of the events leading up to the withdrawal of Ambassadors. It judged that the army and navy commanders were against any military action which might help Sra. Peron's régime to stay in power; and noted that an Argentine Ministry of Foreign Affairs announcement on 8 January that the Argentine Government were going ahead immediately with the extension of the airstrip suggested that they did not wish, at least for the time being, to interfere with communications. It assessed, however, that, although there might be a short lull, further counter-measures against British interests, in the form of more hostile political and economic pressure, were possible in due course. The likelihood of an ' adventurist ' operation had increased. The assessment concluded that military operations remained a more remote possibility but, as the sequence of counter-measures proceeded, must be regarded as that much nearer. An intelligence report of 23 January 1976 referring to a meeting in December 1975 indicated that the armed forces commanders had at that stage ruled out invasion.

RRS Shackleton

42. In December 1975 the British Naval *Attaché* in Buenos Aires had been warned by the Chief of the Argentine Naval Staff that the

---
(¹) *Official Report*, House of Commons, 14 January 1976, Cols. 391–397.

11

C*

RRS Shackleton, an unarmed research ship engaged on a programme of international scientific research unconnected with Lord Shackleton's mission, would be arrested if she entered " Argentine waters " (*i.e.* within 200 miles of the Argentine coast or continental shelf, which in Argentina's view, included the waters surrounding the Falkland Islands). On February 1976 an Argentine destroyer fired shots at the *RRS Shackleton* when she was 78 miles south of Port Stanley, and attempted, unsuccessfully, to arrest her. Subsequent intelligence indicated that plans for the interception had been in existence for about six weeks; that the decision had been taken by the armed forces, not the Government; and that Admiral Massera, the Commander-in-Chief of the Argentine Navy, had authorised firing into the ship but without causing casualties or sinking it. The Joint Intelligence Committee assessed the purpose of the operation as being an assertion of Argentine sovereignty over the Falkland Islands and their surrounding waters, in order to bring pressure to bear on the British Government to negotiate. It also judged that the armed forces commanders were opposed to military invasion, and concluded that the Argentine Government intended to follow a policy of " continued pin-pricks ", which carried the risk of bringing about a progressive deterioration in Anglo-Argentine relations.

Mr. Rowlands's talks in New York

43. On 11 February 1976 Mr. Rowlands, Minister of State at the Foreign and Commonwealth Office, went to New York for talks with the new Argentine Foreign Minister, at which he was instructed by Mr. Callaghan to ask what proposals the Argentines had about discussions on sovereignty and to make it plain that the British Government " would defend the Islands if the Argentines attempted to use force ". Despite the *RRS Shackleton* incident the talks were satisfactory. Mr. Rowlands obtained an assurance that the final leg of the *RRS Shackleton's* programme would not be interfered with; and it was agreed in principle that the dialogue on the Falklands dispute should in due course be resumed.

Defence considerations

44. As explained in paragraph 21, a detachment of Royal Marines has been stationed at Port Stanley since 1965. In addition, over the period an ice-patrol vessel was stationed in the area during the Antarctic summer months, which, in addition to her guardship role, undertook hydrographic and other work in the area of the Falkland Islands and the Dependencies. *HMS Endurance* was brought into service in this capacity in 1967, when she replaced *HMS Protector.* She is armed with two 20 mm Oerlikon guns and carries two Wasp (in 1976 Whirlwind) helicopters equipped with air-to-sea missiles. One consequence of the 1974 Defence Review, which resulted in a phased rundown of overseas commitments outside NATO, was a decision to take *HMS Endurance* out of service. Following the *RRS Shackleton* incident, however, the Secretary of State for Defence, Mr. Roy Mason, agreed to one further deployment of *HMS Endurance.* Following later representations from successive Foreign and Commonwealth Secretaries she was subsequently retained on an annual basis, until 1978, when the Secretary of State for Defence, then Mr. Fred Mulley, agreed to two further deployments, in 1979/80 and 1980/81.

45. In February 1976, in view of the increasing risk of hostile action by Argentina, Mr. Mason agreed to a proposal from Mr. Callaghan for the deployment to the area of a frigate with Royal Fleet Auxiliary([1]) support.

46. In the same month, with a view to discussion in the Defence Committee, Mr. Callaghan asked Mr. Mason for " a full and up-to-date military assessment on possible military options and limitations " considering the range of possible deployments in a number of eventualities, including a determined Argentine assault intended to eject the British garrison. A paper on military options to counter possible Argentine actions was approved by the Chiefs of Staff on 19 February 1976 and circulated as an annex to a paper for the Defence Committee.

47. The Chief of Staffs paper drew attention to the fact that air reinforcement was ruled out by the limitations of the airstrip at Port Stanley; the adverse weather conditions there; its distance from Ascension Island; and the likely unavailability of South American airfields in the event of a conflict. To dislodge Argentine occupation of part of the Falkland Islands or the Dependencies would require an amphibious force with embarked troops. It would not be practicable to provide, transport and support the force necessary in the Islands to ensure that a determined Argentine attempt to eject the British garrison was unsuccessful. To recover the Islands by military means, though far from impossible, would be a major operation at very long range. The least force for this purpose would be of Brigade Group strength, the transport of which would entail the use of all the Navy's amphibious resources, a sizeable Task Force, including *HMS Ark Royal,* and substantial logistic support.

Resumption of negotiations

48. In the light of the deterioration of relations with Argentina, and the agreement in principle reached between Mr. Rowlands and the Argentine Foreign Minister in New York, Mr. Callaghan decided to undertake a major review of policy. In March 1976 the Defence Committee and the Cabinet approved his proposals for a fresh dialogue on all aspects of the dispute, both the possibilities of Anglo-Argentine economic co-operation in the South West Atlantic and " the nature of a hypothetical future constitutional relationship ".

49. Once Argentina had been informed that the Government were prepared to resume negotiations, including discussion of sovereignty, the threat of military action receded. Exploratory talks with Argentina were held in confidence at official level in July and August 1976. By then, following a *coup* on 23 March 1976, Argentina was under the rule of a military Junta, which, with changes in membership, remained in power.

50. In July 1976 the Joint Intelligence Committee assessed the Argentine political situation in the light of events since the military *coup* in March. On the Falklands it concluded that Argentina might have unduly high expectations of the current negotiations. If these were dashed, it could be expected to return to a more aggressive approach, initially in the United Nations. It assessed, however, that it was most unlikely that the Argentine Government would react by taking military action against

([1]) A Royal Fleet Auxiliary is a civilian manned Royal Navy support vessel.

13

the Islands. This assessment derived from intelligence that it was the view of President Videla and others that, if it proved impossible to reach a solution through bilateral negotiations, Argentina would be obliged to seek a solution via the United Nations.

Further Argentine activity at the United Nations

51. In December 1976 the United Nations General Assembly passed another Resolution (31/49 (XXXI)) approving a further report of the Special Committee; expressing " its gratitude for the continuous efforts made by the Government of Argentina . . . to facilitate the process of decolonization and to promote the well-being of the population of the Islands "; and requesting the Governments of Argentina and the United Kingdom to expedite the negotiations and to report to the Secretary-General and to the General Assembly as soon as possible on the results. The Resolution was passed by 102 votes to one (the United Kingdom) with 32 abstentions.

Southern Thule

52. On 20 December 1976 a helicopter from *HMS Endurance* discovered the existence of an Argentine military presence on Southern Thule in the South Sandwich Islands. An intelligence report indicated that the presence was probably established the previous month with the approval of the Naval Commander-in-Chief. On 5 January 1977 the Argentine *Chargé d'Affaires* in London was summoned to the Foreign and Commonwealth Office and asked by the head of the Latin America Department to explain the Argentine presence. At the same time the British *Chargé d'Affaires* in Buenos Aires was instructed to seek an explanation from the Argentine Ministry of Foreign Affairs.

53. On 14 January 1977 the Argentine Ministry of Foreign Affairs delivered a communication to the British *Chargé d'Affaires* in the form of a *bout de papier* claiming that the purpose of the operation was to establish a station with a view to scientific investigation within the jurisdiction of Argentine sovereignty and expressing the hope that nothing would cloud the " auspicious perspectives " for negotiations. The *bout de papier* also stated that the station's permanency would depend on the practicability of the tasks undertaken, although the official delivering it hinted that it would not be permanent. A formal protest was delivered on 19 January 1977 stating that the British Government considered the establishment of the scientific station, without prior reference to the British authorities, a violation of British sovereignty; pointing out that the British Government were entitled to expect that the Argentine Government would have approached them before taking action; and expressing the hope that they would learn that the scientific programme was being terminated. The British Government took no steps to make public the Argentine presence on Southern Thule, which did not become known in the United Kingdom until May 1978.

54. It became clear later in the month that the Argentine presence was larger than the *bout de papier* had indicated. On 27 January 1977 intelligence indicated that the original intention had been to announce the existence of the base in mid or late March, when it was too late for

British ships to enter South Atlantic waters. The Argentine expectation had been that the British reaction would have been stronger. If the Argentine personnel had been captured, the British Antarctic Survey party on South Georgia would have been taken off as a reprisal. According to further intelligence, there was an Argentine Navy contingency plan for a joint air force and navy invasion of the Falkland Islands combined with a diplomatic initiative at the United Nations.

55. The Joint Intelligence Committee assessed the situation on 31 January 1977. It thought it unlikely that the establishment of an Argentine presence on Southern Thule could have been mounted without the approval of the Junta and judged that the Argentine Government's intentions were:

(i) to make a physical demonstration of Argentine sovereignty over the Dependencies;

(ii) to probe the British Government's reaction to such a demonstration; and

(iii) to obtain a bargaining counter in the forthcoming discussions.

The assessment concluded that the Argentine Government were unlikely to order withdrawal until it suited them to do so and, depending on the British Government's actions in the situation, could be encouraged to attempt further military action against British interests in the area.

56. On 7 February 1977 intelligence indicated that the Argentine Navy's contingency plans had been shelved for the time being on the ground that, although an occupation would have had much to commend it for internal political reasons, Argentina could not count on the support of the Third World or the Communist Bloc.

57. On 14 February 1977 *Ultima Clave,* a Buenos Aires weekly political news-sheet, published an article about the occupation of an " island " (Southern Thule) in the South Sandwich Islands. Argentina maintained a presence there and it was still in occupation at the time of the invasion of the Falkland Islands.

Announcement of resumption of negotiations

58. On 2 February 1977 in a statement to Parliament([1]) the Foreign and Commonwealth Secretary, Mr. Crosland, announced the Government's decision that " the time has come to consider both with the Islanders and the Argentine Government whether a climate exists for discussing the broad issues which bear on the future of the Falkland Islands, and the possibilities of co-operation between Britain and Argentina in the region of the South West Atlantic ". He made it clear that in any discussions the Government would reserve their position on sovereignty; that any changes which might be proposed must be acceptable to the Islanders; and that there must be full consultation with the Islanders at every stage. In the same statement, Mr. Crosland announced the Government's conclusions on the recommendations in the Shackleton Report. He said that a number of further studies would be set up, but the Government were not prepared to accept the more costly recommendations, notably the enlargement of the airport and lengthening of the runway. Mr. Crosland reported

([1]) *Official Report,* House of Commons, 2 February 1977, Cols. 550–561.

to the Cabinet the following day that the statement had been received without controversy.

Mr. Rowlands's visit to the Islands and Buenos Aires

59. The Defence Committee approved a proposal by Mr. Crosland that, following his statement, a Foreign and Commonwealth Office Minister should visit the Islands and have talks in Buenos Aires. Before the visit, which was made by Mr. Rowlands, the Joint Intelligence Committee assessed that, if the talks broke down or ended in deadlock, Argentina might decide on military action against British shipping or the Falkland Islands. In the light of this assessment, Foreign and Commonwealth Office and Ministry of Defence officials considered whether any precautionary measures should be taken. Mr. Rowlands was advised that a Royal Navy task group of 6 warships, 3 support ships and a submarine would be in the Atlantic, sailing from Gibraltar to the Caribbean, at the time of the talks. Mr. Rowlands suggested to the Minister of State at the Ministry of Defence that, if, during his discussions with the Argentine Foreign Minister, the Argentines were to threaten the use of force to further their claims in the South-West Atlantic, it might be useful for him to let them know that the task group was in Atlantic waters. Mr. Mulley agreed to this proposal on condition that he was consulted again before reference was made to it. In the event, Mr. Rowlands judged that it was not necessary to refer to the existence of the task group.

60. Mr. Rowlands visited the Islands in February 1977 and held an intensive round of meetings there. The Island Councils agreed to co-operate in working out terms of reference for formal negotiations covering political relations, including sovereignty, and economic co-operation, provided that the talks were covered by the ' sovereignty umbrella ' and that the Islanders were fully consulted. Following Mr. Rowlands's subsequent talks in Buenos Aires and further exchanges, agreement on the terms of reference was reached with Argentina in April 1977 and announced by the new Foreign and Commonwealth Secretary, Dr. Owen, in the House of Commons on 26 April.[1] They were:

" The Governments of the Argentine Republic and the United Kingdom of Great Britain and Northern Ireland have agreed to hold negotiations from June or July 1977 which will concern future political relations, including sovereignty, with regard to the Falkland Islands, South Georgia and South Sandwich Islands, and economic co-operation with regard to the said territories, in particular, and the South West Atlantic, in general.
In these negotiations the issues affecting the future of the Islands will be discussed and negotiations will be directed to the working out of a peaceful solution to the existing dispute on sovereignty between the two states, and the establishment of a framework for Anglo-Argentine economic co-operation which will contribute substantially to the development of the Islands, and the region as a whole.

" A major objective of the negotiations will be to achieve a stable, prosperous and politically durable future for the Islands, whose people the Government of the United Kingdom will consult during the course of the negotiations.

---

[1] *Official Report*, House of Commons, 26 April 1977, Written Answers, Cols. 273–274.

" The agreement to hold these negotiations, and the negotiations themselves, are without prejudice to the position of either Government with regard to sovereignty over the Islands.

" The level at which the negotiations will be conducted, and the times and places at which they will be held, will be determined by agreement between the two Governments. If necessary, special Working Groups will be established."

Talks in Rome

61. Before the first round of talks Dr. Owen presented a paper to the Defence Committee in July 1977, which argued that serious and substantive negotiations were necessary to keep the Argentines in play, since the Islands were militarily indefensible except by a major, costly and unacceptable diversion of current resources. The Committee took the view that it was likely that the Government would be forced back in the end on some variation of a leaseback solution linked with a programme of joint economic co-operation. The aim should be to keep the negotiations with the Argentine Government going so as to allow time for the education of public opinion at home and in the Islands to be carried forward. Broadly speaking, the Government's strategy was to retain sovereignty as long as possible, if necessary making concessions in respect of the Dependencies and the maritime resources in the area, while recognising that ultimately only some form of leaseback arrangement was likely to satisfy Argentina. The talks, which were held at official level, went reasonably well and the options were kept open. The British side put forward the idea that the sovereignty of the uninhabited Dependencies might be looked at separately from the sovereignty of the Falkland Islands themselves.

Threat of Argentine military action

62. Before the next round of talks, conducted by Mr. Rowlands in New York in December 1977, there were several indications that the Argentine position was hardening. In September intelligence indicated that the Argentine Government and Ministry of Foreign Affairs considered that they should take a hard line in the talks as they thought the British were using pretexts to delay progress. At the end of September and the beginning of October 1977 Argentine naval units arrested seven Soviet and two Bulgarian fishing vessels in Falklands waters. An Argentine vessel fired on one of the Bulgarian ships, wounding a Bulgarian sailor. It was known that Admiral Massera's orders were to sink the vessel if necessary. He had also said that there would be a similar riposte to intrusions by any other flag carrier and at any other place. The Argentine Naval *Attaché* in London (Admiral Anaya, who later became Commander-in-Chief of the Navy and a member of the Junta) drew this statement to the attention of the Foreign and Commonwealth Office. On the diplomatic front, the British *Chargé d'Affaires* in Buenos Aires was said to have been subjected to a " barrage of *aides mémoire* and *bouts de papier* " urging the immediate establishment of working groups and other evidence of progress. In addition, the Foreign and Commonwealth Office judged that the failure of the Beagle Channel arbitration—Argentina's other principal foreign policy preoccupation—and its failure to make progress with Brazil in its dispute on the River Plate Basin increased the likelihood of its seeking a success on the Falklands issue.

63. On 11 October 1977 a Joint Intelligence Committee assessment referred to information that another Argentine naval party was due to land on Southern Thule in the middle of the month. It judged that military action was still unlikely pending the negotiations, although Admiral Massera might act unilaterally against a Royal Fleet Auxiliary vessel going to Southern Thule. A fuller assessment on 1 November 1977 referred to the increasing resentment in the Ministry of Foreign Affairs of what were seen as the British Government's delaying tactics; and to the militancy of the Navy. The assessment concluded that the military Junta as a whole would prefer to achieve its sovereignty objectives by peaceful means and that, as long as it calculated that the British Government were prepared to negotiate seriously on the issue of sovereignty, it was unlikely to resort to force. If negotiations broke down, or if Argentina concluded from them that there was no prospect of real progress towards a negotiated transfer of sovereignty, there would be a high risk of its then resorting to more forceful measures, including direct military action. The assessment judged that in those circumstances action against British shipping would be the most serious risk; another possibility was the establishment of an Argentine presence on one or more of the Dependencies, which might involve a risk to the British Antarctic Survey base on South Georgia. A private 'adventurist' operation against the Falklands, which the Junta might feel obliged to support, was always possible. In the Committee's view invasion of the Falkland Islands was unlikely, but could not be discounted.

Consideration of counter-measures

64. In the light of the deteriorating situation, the Foreign and Commonwealth Office asked the Ministry of Defence at the end of October 1977 for a paper on the defence implications of the Argentine threat. The Ministry of Defence circulated a paper on 4 November, which had been approved by the Chiefs of Staff, on the military options to counter possible Argentine actions as identified in the Joint Intelligence Committee's assessment. It followed closely the lines of the paper prepared the previous year (see paragraphs 46–47) and, in relation to the main threats, reached broadly similar conclusions.

65. In the light of the intelligence assessment Ministers decided at a meeting on 21 November 1977 that a military presence in the area of the Falkland Islands should be established by the time the negotiations began in December. The objective would be to buttress the Government's negotiating position by deploying a force of sufficient strength, available if necessary, to convince the Argentines that military action by them would meet resistance. Such a force would not be able to deal with a determined Argentine attack, but it would be able to respond flexibly to limited acts of aggression. The Committee agreed that secrecy should be maintained about the purpose of the force. One nuclear-powered submarine and two frigates were deployed to the area, the submarine to the immediate vicinity of the Islands with the frigates standing off about a thousand miles away. Rules of engagement were drawn up.

66. Cabinet Committee papers show clearly that it was agreed that the force should remain covert. We have found no evidence that the Argentine Government ever came to know of its existence. In the event the negotiations went reasonably well. The Argentine threat receded, and it was agreed after the talks that the naval force could be withdrawn. Consideration

was subsequently given to the possibility of deploying the force again for the next round of negotiations in Lima in February 1978, but Ministers decided not to do so.

Continuation of negotiations to spring 1979

67.   At the negotiations in New York on 13–15 December 1977 it was agreed, in accordance with an earlier Argentine suggestion, to set up two working groups to prepare detailed reports on sovereignty and economic co-operation.   Mr. Rowlands was able to avoid proposing leaseback. Following the meeting Mr. Rowlands went to Rio de Janeiro to brief a delegation of Island Councillors on 18 December on the progress of the talks.

68.   At the talks in Lima in February 1978 the British side proposed an arrangement to provide for British and Argentine scientific activities in the Dependencies, which would have retrospectively legitimised the Argentine presence on Southern Thule.   However, little progress was made at the first meeting of the two working groups, when the Argentine side claimed that the Falklands and Dependencies did not generate a continental shelf; and that the shelf rights therefore belonged to Argentina and were outside the scope of the negotiations.

69.   There were no further formal negotiations until, following Argentine agreement to discuss maritime zones and shelf rights within the negotiations, a meeting at ministerial level was held in December 1978 in Geneva. Mr. Rowlands led the British delegation.   Agreement in principle was reached on a draft co-operation agreement on scientific activities in the Dependencies.   The Falkland Island Councillors, however, when formally consulted about the scheme, rejected it on the ground that, unless restricted to Southern Thule, it would give Argentina a further foothold in the Dependencies, which would start a process leading to eventual loss of sovereignty over the Falkland Islands themselves.   It was explained to the Argentine side at the next round of negotiations held in New York in March 1979 at official level, that, owing to the Falkland Islanders' suspicions of the motives of the Argentine Government, it was not possible to sign the agreement.   Little progress was made at this round of talks.

Significant themes of the period

70.   Without attempting to summarise in any detail the history of the Falkland Islands dispute between 1965 and 1979, we wish to highlight three points:

(i) Successive British Governments sought a solution to the Falkland Islands dispute by negotiation; and they recognised that any solution negotiated with Argentina had to be acceptable to the Islanders.

(ii) The negotiating options gradually narrowed.   The Labour Government made clear in 1977 that sovereignty was an issue for negotiation; but, although transfer of sovereignty combined with leaseback had come to be regarded by the British Government as the most realistic solution, the leaseback proposal was not discussed with Argentina during this period.

(iii) The military threat to the Islands varied in the light of the course of negotiations; it also changed character from 'adventurist' operations in the Islands to wider and more aggressive forms of military action by the Argentine Navy.

19

CHAPTER 2

THE PERIOD OF THE PRESENT GOVERNMENT: MAY 1979 TO 19 MARCH 1982

Re-examination of the options

71. Following the General Election in May 1979 the present Conservative Government took office. Mrs. Thatcher became Prime Minister and Lord Carrington Foreign and Commonwealth Secretary. The Foreign and Commonwealth Office presented the new Minister of State, Mr. Ridley, with a full range of policy options. These were to break off negotiations and be prepared to maintain and defend the Islands against Argentine harassment or worse (' Fortress Falklands '); to give up the Islands, offering to resettle the Islanders elsewhere (which, it was suggested, would be politically and morally indefensible); to go through the motions of negotiations; and to continue the negotiations in good faith in search of a solution which might ultimately prove acceptable to the Islands and Parliament. Mr. Ridley discussed these options with Lord Carrington, and it was agreed that, before the Government decided on the handling of any formal negotiations, Mr. Ridley should visit the Falkland Islands and Argentina to sound out views there at first hand. On 12 June 1979 Mr. Ridley had an exploratory meeting with the Argentine Deputy Foreign Minister, Comodoro Cavandoli. While Mr. Ridley emphasised the Government's interest in economic co-operation with Argentina, Comodoro Cavandoli indicated that his Government would require sovereignty to be a part of any negotiations.

Mr. Ridley's first visit to the Islands and Argentina

72. Mr. Ridley visited the Falkland Islands in July 1979. At meetings with the Islanders he discussed the advantages of co-operation with Argentina, but also made clear that the British Government would not conclude an agreement which did not meet the Islanders' wishes. Informal soundings of Island Councillors' opinion showed a preference for a lengthy ' freeze ' of the dispute and little enthusiasm for the idea of leaseback. Following his visit to the Islands Mr. Ridley had further talks with Comodoro Cavandoli in Buenos Aires, at which agreement was reached on the reinstatement of Ambassadors in Buenos Aires and London. On his departure, however, Mr. Ridley was handed a toughly worded communication in the form of an *aide mémoire* which expressed the Argentine Government's view that negotiations should be resumed " at a more dynamic pace ". The *aide mémoire* referred to the position adopted by the British side at the New York meeting in March 1979 as " a regrettable step backwards "; expressed the hope that an agreement on scientific co-operation could be carried forward in the terms agreed at Geneva the previous year; and reiterated the Argentine position that, while the interests of the Islanders must be taken fully into account, they could not become a third party in negotiations. Mr. Ridley restated the British Government's position that no settlement could be concluded which failed to respect the wishes of the Islanders.

Lord Carrington's proposals

73. On 20 September 1979 Lord Carrington sent a minute to the Prime Minister and other members of the Defence Committee seeking agreement

to a policy towards the Falkland Islands. The minute set out three options: 'Fortress Falklands'; protracted negotiations with no concession on sovereignty; and substantive negotiations on sovereignty. Lord Carrington recommended the last option on the ground that it was in the British interest and that of the Islanders themselves to try to find a way forward through negotiation. He suggested that the solution best fitted to meet the Government's objectives and the wishes of the Islanders would be leaseback, which might be acceptable to the Islanders on the right terms. Continued negotiations would make an unpredictable and possibly violent Argentine reaction less likely. There would, however, be difficulties in carrying out this policy and, if negotiations developed positively, it would be necessary to ensure that it had the support of the Islanders and of Parliament. Lord Carrington asked for agreement to this policy before his meeting the following week in New York with the Argentine Foreign Minister, Brigadier Pastor, at which he hoped to suggest the resumption of negotiations later in the year. After discussion with Lord Carrington, and later with Mr. Ridley, the Prime Minister concluded that a decision of principle on the Government's approach to the problem could not be rushed but should be discussed at an early meeting of the Defence Committee.

74. At the meeting with Lord Carrington in New York Brigadier Pastor proposed a programme of work involving weekly contact between Ambassadors, twice yearly meetings of junior Ministers and an annual meeting of the two Foreign Ministers. Brigadier Pastor said he recognised that the Islands were a long way down in British priorities, but they were at the top of the list for Argentina. Lord Carrington replied that he hoped the difficulties were not insoluble, but that he was not yet in a position to put forward a solution while other pressing foreign policy problems remained outstanding.

75. On 12 October 1979 Lord Carrington circulated a memorandum to the Prime Minister and other members of the Defence Committee with a view to discussion by the Committee at a meeting the following week. The paper restated the options set out in Lord Carrington's minute of 20 September. It pointed out that the 'Fortress Falklands' option and the option of continuing talks but without making any concessions on sovereignty both carried a serious threat of invasion. One of the annexes to the memorandum was a paper on the Argentine political and military threat, which assessed that, if Argentina concluded that there was no prospect of real progress towards a negotiated transfer of sovereignty, there would be a high risk of its resorting to more forceful measures including direct military action. It pointed out that Argentina had the capability to capture the Islands. Lord Carrington recommended that talks with Argentina should be resumed at Ministerial level to explore, without commitment and without seeking to rush matters, political and economic solutions.

76. The Prime Minister decided, however, that discussion of the Falkland Islands by the Defence Committee should be postponed until after the Rhodesian issue had been settled. In November 1979 Mr. Ridley declined an invitation from the Argentine Government for a further informal exchange of views.

21

Assessment of Argentine threat

77. In November 1979 the Joint Intelligence Committee reassessed the Argentine threat to the Falklands. It reviewed developments since the last assessment (in November 1977), since when, as it judged, the Argentine military threat had been diminished by the British Government's decision to negotiate and by Argentina's preoccupation with higher priorities in foreign affairs, notably its dispute with Chile over the Beagle Channel, and with changes in the Argentine Government. It considered, however, that there was no diminution in Argentina's determination to extend its sovereignty to the area of the Falklands, and that the overriding consideration for the Argentine Government remained their perception of the British Government's willingness to negotiate about, and eventually to transfer, sovereignty. It concluded that, while the Argentine Government would prefer to achieve their sovereignty objectives by peaceful means, if negotiations broke down or if for some other reason the Argentine Government calculated that the British Government were not prepared to negotiate seriously on sovereignty, there would be a high risk of their resorting quickly to more forceful measures against British interests; and that in such circumstances direct military action against British shipping or against the Falkland Islands could not be discounted, although " the risk of such action would not be as high as hitherto ".

Exploratory talks

78. On 24 January 1980 Lord Carrington sent a minute to the Prime Minister and other members of the Defence Committee in preparation for a meeting the following week. He advised that exploratory talks with the Argentine Government should be started soon since to continue to stall could be risky. The Defence Committee considered Lord Carrington's memorandum of 12 October 1979 on 29 January 1980. The Committee agreed that it was undesirable that talks should be resumed on the basis of the terms of reference announced by the previous Government in April 1977 (see paragraph 60). It invited Lord Carrington to seek written confirmation from the Falkland Islands Council that it was its wish that talks with the Argentine Government should be resumed; and to propose new terms of reference for them. The agreement of the Falkland Island Councillors was obtained, and it was announced in the House of Commons on 15 April 1980([1]) that talks would take place later that month in New York.

79. The first round of talks was held in New York in April 1980. The British delegation, which was led by Mr. Ridley, included an Island Councillor. The talks were exploratory and, although the Argentine delegation restated the Argentine position on sovereignty, it was agreed that the fundamental difference of opinion on this matter should not inhibit further discussion of the possibility of co-operation in the development and conservation of the resources of the South-West Atlantic.

Leaseback

80. In July 1980 the Defence Committee reviewed the position in the light of these discussions, on the basis of a further memorandum by Lord Carrington. It agreed to attempt to reach a solution of the dispute on the basis of a leaseback arrangement. At a further meeting on

([1]) *Official Report*, House of Commons, 15 April 1980, Written Answers, Col. 589.

7 November the Committee agreed that Mr. Ridley should visit the Islands to discover the level of support there for such an arrangement.

Mr. Ridley's second visit to the Islands

81. Mr. Ridley visited the Falkland Islands again from 22 to 29 November 1980. While in Buenos Aires on his way to the Islands he called on Comodoro Cavandoli. In the Islands Mr. Ridley had a full programme of public and private meetings, at which he put forward several possible future policies, including leaseback. On leaseback Islander opinion appeared to be divided, with a substantial minority opposed to it and the majority undecided.

Parliamentary reaction

82. On his return Mr. Ridley made a statement in the House of Commons on 2 December. It referred to leaseback as one of the possible bases for seeking a negotiated settlement that had been discussed. Although the statement included an assurance that any eventual settlement would have to be endorsed by the Islanders, and by Parliament, it received a very hostile reception from all sides of the House.([1]) Ministers considered the views of the Islanders and the reaction of Parliament at a meeting of the Defence Committee on 3 December 1980, and in Cabinet the following day. The Cabinet noted that this was a highly emotive issue for Parliamentary and public opinion in Britain, where the Islanders' hostility to Mr. Ridley's approach seemed to have been exaggerated: it would be tragic if the Islands' chances of escaping from economic blight were to be diminished by the attitude of their champions at Westminster.

Islander reaction

83. On 6 January 1981 the Falkland Islands Joint Councils passed a motion in the following terms:

" While this House does not like any of the ideas put forward by Mr. Ridley for a possible settlement of the sovereignty dispute with Argentina, it agrees that Her Majesty's Government should hold further talks with the Argentines at which this House should be represented and at which the British delegation should seek an agreement to freeze the dispute over sovereignty for a specified period of time."

Opening of formal negotiations

84. The Defence Committee reviewed the position on 29 January 1981 on the basis of a memorandum by Lord Carrington. He judged that, in withholding support for leaseback, the Island Councils' response was less than had been hoped for; but they had given a mandate for future talks, although the idea of a freeze of the dispute was unlikely to be acceptable to the Argentines. In his view the aim should be to keep negotiations going; and, while applying no pressure, to let the Islanders come to see the need to explore a realistic settlement based on leaseback. Lord Carrington recommended that the Government should agree to early talks, for which Argentina was pressing, before the change of government there in March. The Defence Committee endorsed Lord Carrington's recommendations.

([1]) The text of Mr. Ridley's statement and the subsequent exchanges is reproduced in Annex F.

85. Talks were held in New York in February 1981: Mr. Ridley led the British side, which included two Falkland Islands Councillors. Mr. Ridley proposed a 'freeze' of the dispute, which was rejected outright by the Argentine side.

86. On 13 March 1981 Lord Carrington sent a minute to the Prime Minister and other members of the Defence Committee reporting the outcome of these talks. He said that, although the Argentines had rejected the 'freeze' proposal, the talks had been helpful education for both the Islanders attending them and the Argentines, and had narrowed the issues. Lord Carrington saw little point in further talks until the Islanders had cleared their own minds. He considered that, if in the end the Islanders decided that they would prefer the *status quo,* it would be necessary to prepare for the possibility of a deterioration of relations with Argentina, which might involve supplying the Islands, if Argentina withdrew its services, and perhaps defending them against physical harassment.

87. Following a press conference given by the Falkland Island Councillors on their return home from the talks in New York, Foreign and Commonwealth Office officials advised Mr. Ridley on 26 March 1981 that there were grounds for cautious optimism about eventually being given a mandate to develop negotiations, but expressed concern that the timetable envisaged by Island Councillors for reaching a decision would be unacceptable to Argentina. It was unlikely that the Councillors would begin to consider the issues until their elections in the autumn at the earliest. At the beginning of May 1981 the British Ambassador in Buenos Aires wrote to the Foreign and Commonwealth Office strongly urging at least one further round of talks during the year, including discussion of sovereignty, in order to avoid a deterioration of relations with Argentina. The Foreign and Commonwealth Office replied that they were under no illusions about the limits of Argentine patience or the risk of serious confrontation if the British Government appeared unwilling or unable to continue substantive negotiations on sovereignty. However, substantive negotiations without the approval of the Islanders ran up against the Government's public commitment to the principle that the wishes of the Islanders were paramount, on which Parliament had strong views. If Argentina chose to exert pressure, as might be expected, it would be necessary to deal with the situation as it arose, but always with the proviso that Islander wishes were paramount. It was decided to send a senior official (Mr. J. B. Ure, the Assistant Under-Secretary of State concerned) to visit the Falkland Islands, in order to encourage an early decision, and to visit Argentina to reassure the Argentine Government of the British Government's wish to make progress towards a solution and to seek to persuade them not to force the pace.

Argentine views

88. One indication of Argentine impatience at lack of progress in the talks was a speech made on 29 May 1981 (Army Day in Argentina) by General Galtieri, then the Army Commander-in-Chief, in which he said:

> " Neither are we prepared to allow those who are discussing with us the return of island territories that are Argentine by historical inheritance and legal right to interfere in the slightest way with the search for and exploitation of the wealth of our continental shelf.

24

" Nobody can or will be able to say that we have not been extremely calm and patient in our handling of international problems, which in no way stem from any appetite for territory on our part. However, after a century and a half they [these problems] are becoming more and more unbearable."

89. On 15 June 1981 Mr. Ridley had a general discussion of the Falklands issue in Paris with the new Argentine Deputy Foreign Minister, Sr. Ros. The Argentines appeared to be reconciled to awaiting the results of the Falkland Islands Council elections, but were concerned that the results might foreclose the options; they feared that the generally negative and critical attitude of the Islanders towards Argentine efforts to improve relations by providing air and fuel services might cause domestic opinion in Argentina to conclude that there was no value in positive gestures or even in continuing negotiations.

Mr. Ridley's office meeting on 30 June 1981

90. On 30 June 1981 a major review of policy was undertaken in the Foreign and Commonwealth Office at a meeting chaired by Mr. Ridley, which was attended by, among others, Sir Michael Palliser, the Permanent Under-Secretary of State; Mr. D. M. Day, the Deputy Under-Secretary of State concerned; Mr. A. J. Williams, H.M. Ambassador in Buenos Aires; Mr. R. M. Hunt (as he then was), the Governor of the Falkland Islands; Mr. J. B. Ure, the Superintending Assistant Under-Secretary of State for the South America Department; and Mr. P. R. Fearn, the Head of the South America Department. The meeting had before it a paper prepared by Mr. Ure following his visit to Argentina and the Falkland Islands earlier in the month. In the paper Mr. Ure said that he had " found Argentine Foreign Affairs Ministers and officials reasonably relaxed about progress—or lack of progress—on the Falklands negotiations and well disposed towards the leaseback idea ". They had warned, however, that the military leaders were " less patient and might require a more ' forward ' policy at any time ". In the Islands Mr. Ure had formed the impression that opinion had not hardened irrevocably against leaseback; but he judged that, in order to secure agreement to it, much more would need to be done to educate Islander and United Kingdom opinion about the danger of inaction and the safeguards on which the Government would insist in any leaseback arrangements. He suggested a number of measures to assist a campaign of public education, including assurances to the Islanders on access to the United Kingdom, a resettlement scheme for those dissatisfied with any arrangements reached, further land distribution schemes, and the initiation of more productive economic schemes for the Islands. He recommended that, if such an approach were considered unacceptable, consideration should be given to preparing fuller contingency plans for the defence and development of the Islands.

91. In preparation for the meeting the British Ambassador in Buenos Aires had also set out his views, in a telegram on 10 June 1981. He said that ground had been lost since February both because it was less possible to depend on continued Argentine patience and understanding and because Islander opinion of the realities of the situation had been allowed to slide back. If the only practicable outcome was some form of negotiated leaseback, it was apparent that acceptance of that conclusion would not

come of itself in the Islands, in Parliament or even in the whole of Government. The Ambassador recommended that the forthcoming meeting should concentrate on the possibility of a " sales campaign ", perhaps mainly by bringing home to British opinion the potential cost of any alternative. He warned that the risk of Argentina's using Britain as a scapegoat for its domestic troubles could well be much more threatening by the end of the year. If the Government sponsored more visibly the idea that a negotiated settlement must be envisaged and achieved, it would help to reduce the risk of Argentina's concluding that the Government were simply bamboozling them without any basic intention of reaching a mutually acceptable settlement.

92. At the meeting on 30 June the situation in Argentina and in the Islands was also discussed in detail. The Governor gave the view from the Islands. He said that the Islanders wished to have nothing whatsoever to do with the Argentines; they did not believe that any terms which could be agreed for a leaseback settlement could ever provide them with the guarantees that they wanted.

93. The conclusions reached by the meeting were that the immediate aim should be to play for time with Argentina; that the new Falkland Islands Legislative Council, when elected, should be persuaded to allow talks to continue; that a paper for the Defence Committee should be prepared recommending a major public education campaign; and that up-to-date contingency papers, both civil and military, should be prepared as annexes to it.

Intelligence assessment

94. On 9 July 1981 the Joint Intelligence Committee circulated a new assessment of the likelihood of Argentina's resorting over the next few months to forcible action in the Falkland Islands dispute. It reviewed developments since the last assessment in 1979, including the progress of talks held with Argentina in that period, political and economic developments in Argentina, the progress of its sovereignty dispute with Chile about islands in the Beagle Channel and its improving relations with the United States and Brazil. The assessment reviewed the options open to the Argentine Government if they decided to resort to direct measures in the dispute. It took the view that it was likely that in the first instance Argentina would adopt diplomatic and economic measures. The latter could include the disruption of air and sea communications, of food and oil supplies and of the provision of medical treatment. There was also a distinct possibility that Argentina might occupy one of the uninhabited Dependencies, following up its action in 1976 in establishing a presence on Southern Thule; and a risk that it might establish a military presence in the Falkland Islands themselves, remote from Port Stanley. In the Committee's view harassment or arrest of British shipping would not be a likely option unless the Argentine Government felt themselves severely provoked.

95. As in 1979, the assessment noted that there was no sign of diminution in Argentina's determination eventually to extend its sovereignty over the Falkland Islands area, but that it would prefer to achieve this objective by peaceful means and would turn to forcible action only as a last resort. As before, it judged that the overriding consideration would be Argentina's perception of the Government's willingness to negotiate genuinely about,

and eventually to transfer, sovereignty. It recorded evidence of impatience in Argentina at the absence of progress in negotiations and at the attitude of the Islanders. Earlier in the year Argentina had reduced the scheduled flights to the Islands and delayed a supply ship. These actions were seen as evidence that in any escalation of the dispute such measures would be likely to come first. It was thought, however, that relatively small-scale military action could not be ruled out. The final paragraph of the assessment stated that, if Argentina concluded that there was no hope of a peaceful transfer of sovereignty, there would be a high risk of its resorting to more forcible measures against British interests, and that it might act swiftly and without warning. In such circumstances military action against British shipping or a full-scale invasion of the Falkland Islands could not be discounted.

Mr. Ridley's report to Lord Carrington

96. On 20 July Mr. Ridley sent a minute to Lord Carrington. He recorded the agreement of his meeting on 30 June that there was no alternative to the leaseback idea which stood any chance of solving the dispute, while noting that the prospects for negotiating a sovereignty solution with Islander agreement had receded in recent months. The forthcoming general elections in the Islands seemed certain to lead to a new Legislative Council opposed to substantive sovereignty talks with Argentina. While it might be possible to manage one more round of talks without specific sovereignty proposals on the table, it must be expected that Argentine patience would then run out. Mr. Ridley warned that, if Argentina concluded, possibly by early 1982, that the Government were unable or unwilling to negotiate seriously, retaliatory action must be expected: in the first instance through the withdrawal of communications, fuel and other facilities which it provided; in the longer run through some form of military action. Mr. Ridley then examined the options available. He dismissed that of simply playing for time, except in the very short term, and suggested that there were three possible courses of action: to open negotiations on leaseback with or without Islander concurrence or participation, but with the outcome remaining conditional on the agreement of the Islanders and of Parliament; to embark on a public education campaign to educate Islander and British public opinion about the facts of the situation, the consequences of a failure to negotiate and the corresponding advantages of a sovereignty solution; or to let Argentina conclude that the Government would not discuss sovereignty, and to set in hand contingency action to deal with the consequences. Mr. Ridley advised against the first of these on the ground that it would breach the long held policy of acting only in accordance with the Islanders' wishes; and the third on the ground that it would be difficult and very costly to sustain the Islands and could lead to a military confrontation with Argentina. He recommended adopting the second option, despite the public criticism that it was likely to attract, and suggested that the matter should be discussed in the Defence Committee in September.

Formal expression of Argentine views

97. On 27 July 1981 a note was delivered to the British Ambassador in Buenos Aires from the Argentine Foreign Minister, Dr. Camilion, expressing the Argentine Government's serious concern at the lack of progress at the last round of talks in February 1981. It referred to the fact that ten years had passed since the Communications Agreements and stated

27

that in the Argentine Government's view it was not possible:

"to postpone further a profound and serious discussion of the complex essential constituents of the negotiations—sovereignty and economic co-operation—in a simultaneous and global fashion with the express intention of achieving concrete results shortly. A resolute impetus must therefore be given to the negotiations. The next round of negotiations cannot be another mere exploratory exercise, but must mark the beginning of a decisive stage towards the definitive termination of the dispute."

The Argentine Ministry of Foreign Affairs issued a simultaneous *communiqué* referring to the note, rehearsing Argentina's claim and stating that the Argentine Government considered that " the acceleration of negotiations on the Malvinas, with resolution and with clear objectives in view, had become an unpostponable priority for its foreign policy ". The *communiqué* expressed the Argentine Government's determination to continue the negotiations " in an eminently realistic spirit and with the full certainty that there are rational and attainable solutions "; and concluded, " there is a national awareness of the problem, which on the one hand allows for negotiation and which on the other believes that it is not possible to defer this question which affects territorial integrity and national dignity ".

Lord Carrington's decision

98. On 7 September 1981 Lord Carrington discussed the position with the Lord Privy Seal (Sir Ian Gilmour), Mr. Ridley and officials. A draft Defence Committee paper was prepared for consideration at the meeting. It drew attention to the increasing urgency of finding a solution to the dispute and set out the options in similar terms to Mr. Ridley's minute to Lord Carrington, recommending, as he had, a much more public and active campaign to educate Islander and British public opinion.

99. Lord Carrington did not accept this course of action. As, in accordance with normal Foreign and Commonwealth Office practice, no minutes of the meeting were taken, the reasons for his decision were not recorded at the time. But Lord Carrington told us that, in his view, such a campaign would not have been agreed to by his colleagues and would have been counter-productive. In a personal letter to the British Ambassador in Buenos Aires on 23 September, Mr. Fearn, the Head of the South America Department, explained that Ministers had decided that " the domestic political constraints must at this stage continue to prevent us from taking any steps which might be interpreted either as putting pressure on the Islanders or as overruling their wishes. Specifically that meant that an education campaign in the Islands and the United Kingdom has, at least for the present, been ruled out ". In oral evidence Sir Michael Palliser, the Permanent Under-Secretary of State at the time, told us that, according to his recollection, it was decided that it was not an appropriate time for Ministers to discuss the matter collectively in the Defence Committee, because of, among other things, the absence of any immediate danger of hostile Argentine reactions.

100. But, although he did not seek a meeting, Lord Carrington sent a minute to the Prime Minister and to other members of the Defence Committee on 14 September 1981, in advance of discussing the dispute with Dr. Camilion at the United Nations General Assembly in New York later that month. In it he referred to the Argentine note and *communiqué,* which

had been circulated at the United Nations, and expressed his conviction that leaseback still provided the most likely, and perhaps the only, basis for an agreed solution of the dispute. He noted, however, that the prospects for negotiating such a solution with Islander agreement had diminished and, given the Islanders' views, there was little prospect of doing more than keeping some sort of negotiation with Argentina going. Putting pressure on the Islanders to take any decisions against their will could only be counter-productive. Lord Carrington proposed to tell Dr. Camilion that the British Government wanted to end the dispute, but that they could act only in accordance with the wishes of the Islanders, and to invite the Argentine Government to put forward constructive proposals of their own. He recognised, however, that this would be unwelcome to the Argentine Government and that, if they concluded that the British Government were unable or unwilling to negotiate seriously, they might see little purpose in trying to maintain a dialogue. This could lead to the withdrawal of the Islands' air service and a significant part of their fuel supply. The risk of ultimately becoming involved in a military confrontation with Argentina could not be discounted. Lord Carrington explained that contingency studies were being undertaken by officials (see paragraphs 108 *et seq*), but that it was clear that supplying and defending the Islands would be both difficult and costly.

Lord Carrington's meeting with Dr. Camilion in New York

101   On 22 September 1981 Dr. Camilion addressed the United Nations General Assembly. He referred to the " present illegal occupation " of the Islands and expressed his Government's hope that they would be " able to report in due course to the General Assembly that this series of negotiations concerning the Malvinas, South Georgia and South Sandwich Islands, which we hope will begin soon, was the last one ".

102.   Lord Carrington met Dr. Camilion the following day. The relevant telegram reported that he had told him that the British Government wanted negotiations, but, although they would continue to do their best to persuade the Islanders of the benefits of an accommodation, they could not seek to coerce them. Lord Carrington suggested that it would be preferable if Argentina put forward proposals when talks resumed. Dr. Camilion emphasised that the key question was that of sovereignty, which had to be negotiated between the United Kingdom and Argentina. The Islanders could not be allowed to veto the resumption of negotiations.

103.   Argentine press comment after the meeting, based on a press conference that Dr. Camilion gave, presented the talks as a most significant development in the Falklands negotiations, with Britain agreeing for the first time with Argentina that the present status of the Islands could not be maintained. Dr. Camilion was reported as having emerged visibly satisfied from the talks. He was quoted in the Argentine press as saying that " Lord Carrington advanced to the point of saying that the present *status quo* is difficult to sustain today ".

The views of the British Ambassador in Buenos Aires

104.   When he was informed of Lord Carrington's decision not to pursue a public education campaign, the British Ambassador in Buenos Aires

29

protested strongly in a letter to Mr. Fearn on 2 October 1981. He said that, as he understood it, the decision was to have no strategy at all beyond a general Micawberism. It had to be recognised that the " unguided ' wishes of the Falkland Islanders ' were very, very unlikely in any foreseeable future to provide even a grudging acceptance of sovereignty transfer in any form ". There was a clear risk that the Argentines would conclude that talking was a waste of time. The Ambassador said that " talks for the sake of talking " were something the Argentines conceded to the British and not *vice versa;* and he was dubious about their being ready to concede them any longer. If it was no longer possible to negotiate meaningfully about sovereignty, it would be better to tell the Argentines frankly and face the consequences.

Dr. Camilion's view of negotiations

105. Dr. Camilion discussed his ideas for negotiations with the British Ambassador in Buenos Aires at some length on 14 October 1981. He said that, for serious and constructive negotiations, it was necessary to tackle all the component parts of what was a complex issue. There would be a need to establish a methodology and draw up a catalogue of the subjects to be covered, and then to examine them piecemeal, even if the final settlement had to be concluded globally. Dr. Camilion recognised that meaningful negotiations would have to be long and difficult. These remarks were welcomed in the Foreign and Commonwealth Office as indicating Argentine acceptance that no early solution was obtainable and reluctance on their part to move to confrontation. While it was recognised that there was no weakening in the Argentine Government's ultimate and overriding objective of securing a transfer of sovereignty, their position as stated by Dr. Camilion was seen as offering scope for a protracted dialogue.

Falkland Islands Elections

106. The elections to the Falkland Islands Legislative Council were completed on 14 October 1981 and, as expected, reflected a hardening of Islanders' attitudes against negotiations on sovereignty. The new Legislative Council agreed, however, to the need to keep a dialogue going, provided that sovereignty was not on the agenda. It supported a proposal to send representatives to further talks with Argentina, which were originally arranged to be held in Geneva on 17 and 18 December 1981. Because of the change of Government in Buenos Aires Argentina asked for the talks to be postponed until January 1982; they were then further postponed until the end of February because of Mr. Luce's[1] other commitments, in particular in connection with the Canada Bill.

107. On 2 December 1981 Lord Carrington sent a further minute to the Prime Minister and other members of the Defence Committee, referring to his meeting with Dr. Camilion and the outcome of the Falkland Islands elections. He noted that Argentine and Islander attitudes left little room for manoeuvre at the next round of negotiations, and that it would be left to the Argentine side to make the running. Lord Carrington said that he could not be optimistic on the outcome of the talks, but there was some hope that they would not end in a complete stalemate. The Argentines were likely to press for parallel working groups on economic co-operation and on sovereignty, and in this event the aim would be to seek to persuade the

---

[1] Mr. Luce had succeeded Mr. Ridley as Minister of State in September 1981.

Island Councillors to agree that the establishment of the latter group would not involve any surrender of their rights. Lord Carrington also referred to the possible need to provide alternative services, based on sea rather than air communication, at an initial cost of about £6 million, if Argentina withdrew its services.

Contingency planning and HMS Endurance

Civil contingency plans

108. Early in 1981 the Foreign and Commonwealth Office, which was responsible for initiating civil contingency plans for the Islands, had begun to look at what could be done in the event of Argentina's withdrawing the services it provided. In May 1981 Foreign and Commonwealth Office officials consulted the Overseas Development Administration about the possibility of extending the runway at Port Stanley to accommodate long haul jets; the provision of alternative sea communications; and the cost of providing better medical facilities. The Civil Aviation Authority provided estimates of the cost of extending the runway to different lengths. The Department of Trade was consulted about the feasibility of various forms of sea service. The outcome of these consultations was a note by officials prepared in September 1981 as an annex to the draft paper for the Defence Committee, which was considered at Lord Carrington's meeting on 7 September (see paragraph 98). The note concluded that an alternative air service was likely to be impracticable. The only country from which such a service could be provided without extension of the runway at Port Stanley was Chile. It would need to be extended to 7,000 feet to accommodate aircraft from Uruguay or Brazil, at an estimated cost of about £11 million at 1981 prices. It was unlikely, however, that South American countries would be prepared to allow the provision of alternative air services, in which case the runway would need to be extended to 10,000–12,000 feet to accommodate long haul aircraft from South Africa at a cost of about £16 million. A far more sophisticated airport would also be required. Even then there would be difficulties, as Argentina could refuse to allow Argentine airfields to be designated as alternatives to Port Stanley if an aircraft needed to divert. It was likely, therefore, to be possible to provide only a sea service. The cost of a charter would be of the order of about £8,000 a day. Consideration was also given to the need to prepare alternative means of providing the Islands with fuel and of transporting freight and to the effects of Argentina's withdrawing its educational facilities and emergency medical service.

Military contingency planning

109. Earlier in the year the Foreign and Commonwealth Office had also asked the Ministry of Defence to update the assessment prepared in 1977 (see paragraph 64) of what could be done to counter military action by Argentina. Some explanation of nomenclature is required here. The former Chief of the Defence Staff (Lord Lewin) explained to us that in military terminology 'contingency planning' has a precise meaning. It is a form of planning that leads to the preparation of a Joint Theatre Plan. A Joint Theatre Plan is a detailed plan to meet a specified contingency, usually one requiring air reinforcement. It is prepared on the instructions of the Chiefs of Staff and is regularly reviewed and updated. The papers prepared at various times by the Ministry of Defence at the request of the

Foreign and Commonwealth Office were not contingency plans in this sense, but a much broader appreciation of the action that would be necessary to counter various forms of military action by Argentina. They did, however, incorporate a 'concept of operations', on which military action could be based.

110. At a meeting between Ministry of Defence and Foreign and Commonwealth Office officials on 1 May 1981 it was agreed that what was required was a " short politico-military assessment of the United Kingdom's ability to respond militarily to a range of possible Argentine actions, the implications of responding in a particular way and the chances of success, with some indication of the possible cost ". (It was also agreed that plans for the evacuation of the Island population in the event of an emergency should not be prepared.) It was envisaged that the paper would form an annex to a paper for the Defence Committee. On completion the paper was formally approved by the Chiefs of Staff on 14 September 1981.

111. This paper, which was similar in scope to that prepared in 1977, examined the military options identified by the July 1981 Joint Intelligence Committee assessment as open to Argentina and possible responses to them. It noted that Argentina had some of the most efficient armed forces in South America, and gave a brief account of its naval and air capability. It also drew attention to Britain's very limited military capability in the area, consisting of only the garrison of 42 lightly armed Royal Marines on the Islands, the part-time Falkland Islands' defence force, and *HMS Endurance,* which was due to be withdrawn in March 1982. The paper explained that the length of the runway at Port Stanley, the lack of diversion airfields, the limited airfield facilities and the adverse and unpredictable weather conditions precluded air reinforcement on any significant scale. A British military response would therefore have to be primarily a naval one. Passage time was of the order of 20 days for surface ships, and additional time would be required to assemble and prepare sea reinforcements, which could involve significant penalties to other military commitments.

112. The paper then examined possible responses to various forms of Argentine action: harassment or arrest of British shipping; military occupation of one or more of the uninhabited islands; arrest of the British Antarctic Survey team on South Georgia; a small-scale military operation against the Islands; and full-scale military invasion of the Islands. On the last option the paper judged that, to deter a full-scale invasion, a large balanced force would be required, comprising an Invincible class carrier with four destroyers or frigates, plus possibly a nuclear-powered submarine, supply ships in attendance and additional manpower up to brigade strength, to reinforce the garrison. Such a deployment would be very expensive and would engage a significant portion of the country's naval resources. There was a danger that its despatch could precipitate the very action it was intended to deter. If then faced with Argentine occupation of the Falkland Islands on arrival, there could be no certainty that such a force could retake them. The paper concluded that to deal with a full-scale invasion would require naval and land forces with organic air support on a very substantial scale, and that the logistic problems of such an operation would be formidable.

113. In the period that the Chiefs of Staff paper was being prepared there was some anxiety in the Ministry of Defence (Navy Department)

about the lack of detailed contingency plans for the protection of the Falkland Islands themselves and of the Royal Marine platoon there. The United Kingdom Commanders-in-Chief's Committee gave further consideration to the matter in February 1982, when the Assistant Chief of the Defence Staff (Operations) reported that, pending consideration of the Chiefs of Staff paper by the Defence Committee, there was no enthusiasm in the Ministry of Defence for detailed contingency planning. Since these discussions at the planning level were not carried to the point of consideration by the Chiefs of Staff at that stage, we do not regard them as significant for our review, particularly in the light of the evidence given to us by the former Chief of Defence Staff, to which we referred in paragraph 109.

HMS Endurance

114. One consequence of the 1981 Defence Review was the decision to withdraw *HMS Endurance* at the end of her 1981–82 deployment. Lord Carrington wrote to the Secretary of State for Defence, Mr. Nott, on 5 June 1981 on several aspects of the defence programme, including the withdrawal of *HMS Endurance*. He pressed for her retention on the ground that, until the dispute with Argentina was settled, it was important to maintain the British Government's normal presence in the area at the current level; any reduction would be interpreted by both the Islanders and Argentina as a reduction in Britain's commitment to the Islands and in its willingness to defend them. Lord Carrington also pointed out that the hydrographic survey tasks *HMS Endurance* undertook and the operation of her helicopters over a wide area of the British Antarctic Territory were an important aspect of the maintenance of the British claim to sovereignty. Although *HMS Endurance* was nearing the end of her normal working life, it was essential that she should be replaced by a vessel of similar type for Antarctic work. This approach was followed up by a meeting of officials on 10 June 1981, following which Foreign and Commonwealth Office officials judged that there was no prospect of the decision being reversed, and so reported to Mr. Ridley. The decision to withdraw *HMS Endurance* was confirmed in Parliament on 30 June 1981.([1])

115. When they were informed of the decision, the Falkland Islands Councils held a joint meeting on 26 June 1981, following which they sent a message to Lord Carrington in the following terms:

"The people of the Falkland Islands deplore in the strongest terms the decision to withdraw *HMS Endurance* from service. They express extreme concern that Britain appears to be abandoning its defence of British interests in the South Atlantic and Antarctic at a time when other powers are strengthening their position in these areas. They feel that such a withdrawal will further weaken British sovereignty in this area in the eyes not only of Islanders but of the world. They urge that all possible endeavours be made to secure a reversal of this decision".

116. In July 1981 the British Embassy in Buenos Aires reported, in a letter to the Foreign and Commonwealth Office at official level, that several Argentine newspapers had carried prominently versions of a report

(1) *Official Report*, House of Lords, 30 June 1981, Col. 185.

of an article in *The Daily Telegraph* on the subject. The letter reported that all the newspaper articles highlighted the theme that Britain was " abandoning the protection of the Falkland Islands ". An intelligence report in September 1981 quoted an Argentine diplomatic view that the withdrawal of *HMS Endurance* had been construed by the Argentines as a deliberate political gesture; they did not see it as an inevitable economy in Britain's defence budget since the implications for the Islands and for Britain's position in the South Atlantic were fundamental.

117. Lord Carrington wrote again to Mr. Nott on 22 January 1982 referring to the protests that the news of *HMS Endurance's* withdrawal had aroused. He referred to an Early Day Motion in the House of Commons that had been signed by over 150 MPs, and to a debate in the House of Lords on 16 December 1981 that had centred on the decision.[1] Lord Carrington said that the decision was being interpreted as a stage in a deliberate British policy of reducing support for the Falkland Islands; and as demonstrating a lack of commitment to Britain's sovereignty, and to the related economic potential, in Antarctica. He suggested a discussion of the matter. Mr. Nott replied on 3 February 1982 declining to reverse the decision. He argued that the Government were on reasonable grounds as regards their commitments in the Falklands as they would be keeping the Royal Marine garrison there at its present strength. Royal Naval ships would continue to visit periodically, though less frequently than *HMS Endurance*. In answer to a question in the House of Commons on 9 February 1982 about the future of *HMS Endurance*[2] the Prime Minister said that the decision to withdraw her had been very difficult and that, in view of the competing claims on the defence budget and the defence capability of *HMS Endurance*, the Secretary of State for Defence had decided that other claims on the budget should have greater priority.

118. Lord Carrington wrote to Mr. Nott again on 17 February 1982 expressing his continued concern at the strength of public and Parliamentary opposition to *HMS Endurance's* withdrawal and at the consequence for the Government's position on the Falklands. He said that he did not wish to rule out an approach to the Defence Committee for additional finance, but suggested that it would be better to wait until the outcome of the talks in New York on 26 and 27 February 1982, when Argentine intentions and the defence implications would be clearer.

Events leading up to the New York talks

General Galtieri's accession

119. General Galtieri succeeded President Viola as President of Argentina on 22 December 1981. He was in a stronger position than his predecessors since he also retained his position as Commander-in-Chief of the Army, which he was due to hold until the end of 1982. It is also significant, in view of the traditional inter-service rivalry in Argentina, that he is said to have been a personal friend of Admiral Anaya, the Commander-in-Chief of the Navy. The British Ambassador in Buenos Aires reported at the time that the Argentine Navy, traditionally the hardest of the services on the Falklands issue, was playing a decisive role in the change of Government, which it was likely to maintain in the new Junta.

---

[1] *Official Report*, House of Lords, 16 December 1981, Cols. 209–237.
[2] *Official Report*, House of Commons, 9 February 1982, Col. 856.

120. General Galtieri took office at a time of improving relations with the United States. 1981 had been marked by a number of high level visits between the United States and Argentina. President Reagan's personal emissary, General Vernon Walters, had visited Argentina in February and September; the United States Army Commander-in-Chief, General Meyer, in April and the United States Ambassador to the United Nations, Mrs. Kirkpatrick, in August. General Viola had visited the United States in March and General Galtieri had himself paid two visits there, in August at the invitation of General Meyer, and in October for the inter-American Conference of Army Commanders-in-Chief.

121. In the new Government Dr. Nicanor Costa Mendez, who had previously been Foreign Minister in the Government of President Ongania from 1966 to 1969 (at the time of negotiations between the United Kingdom and Argentina on the ' Memorandum of Understanding '), was appointed Foreign Minister in place of Dr. Camilion. The Foreign and Commonwealth Office view of the implications of the new Government for the Falklands dispute was that the basic Argentine position was unlikely to change, but a more forceful approach could be expected. In his inaugural speech to the nation on 23 December 1981 President Galtieri made no mention of the dispute, although he had, as noted in paragraph 88, made a reference to it in strong terms in a speech the previous May.

The situation at the beginning of the year

122. On 1 January 1982 the British Ambassador in Buenos Aires submitted his Annual Review for 1981. He noted that the Ministers chosen by the new President were a great improvement on their predecessors. 1981 had been a difficult year for relations between Britain and Argentina, mainly on account of the Falklands dispute. He said, " we have come through without a bust-up, but certainly with the Argentines and the Islanders more on each other's nerves than a year ago ". In submitting to Mr. Ure and Mr. Luce a draft reply to the Ambassador, Mr. Fearn observed that, while they had managed to avoid matters developing into a confrontation, they would be fortunate to do so for a further year unless Islanders' attitudes changed. In his reply to the Ambassador on 28 January 1982 Mr. Fearn made the point that, unless the Islanders modified their attitudes, which was unlikely, it was going to be increasingly difficult to persuade the Argentines of the virtues of continuing to seek a solution by negotiation.

123. On 19 January 1982 the Governor of the Falkland Islands submitted his Annual Review for 1981. He noted that the Islanders' relations with both Britain and Argentina had deteriorated during the year. Islander opinion had hardened against leaseback. Their suspicions of the Government's intentions had been increased by a number of unconnected matters, including the refusal to grant British citizenship to Falkland Islanders in the British Nationality Bill, the announcement of the withdrawal of *HMS Endurance*, and financial cuts in the British Antarctic Survey, especially the threatened closure of its base at Grytviken in South Georgia. A large number of Argentine actions had antagonised the Islanders, in particular the reduction at very short notice in the frequency of the air service and the fact that there had been six overflights by Argentine Air Force aircraft. The elections had led to a Legislative Council on which the

35

F*

elected members were unanimously opposed to leaseback. In consequence the Governor saw no way ahead in future talks, as long as Argentina continued to insist upon sovereignty first and the British Government continued to maintain that Islander wishes were paramount. He thought that, if talks broke down, the first step that Argentina would take would be to stop the air service, and he discussed various measures that would be necessary to meet that contingency and other action of a similar kind that Argentina might take.

124. In a detailed analysis of the Review, which he submitted to Mr. Ure and Mr. Luce, Mr. Fearn observed that in 1981 the leaseback initiative had run into the ground and the Islanders had moved to open support of a 'Fortress Falklands' policy. Leaseback was now " effectively dead "; its demise meant that " we are left with no alternative way to prevent the dispute moving sooner or later to more open confrontation ".

125. A formal reply, approved by Mr. Luce, was sent to the Governor by Mr. Ure on 4 March. In it he confirmed the Governor's pessimistic analysis of the future of the dispute and commented that, given Argentine and Islander attitudes, " we are now perilously near the inevitable move from dialogue to confrontation ". It was explained to us in evidence that the word " confrontation " was not intended to mean primarily military confrontation, and that the purpose of the letter was in part to serve as a warning to the Islanders, through the Governor, of the consequences of a breakdown in negotiations. The reply pointed out that the range of options open to the Argentines went far wider than a withdrawal of present services. It had to be recognised that for the British Government it would be difficult not only to find the necessary finance but also, in the final analysis, to defend the Islands and the Dependencies in any adequate way. It would be necessary to carry forward the contingency planning already undertaken against a withdrawal of services. It was unlikely to be possible to provide an alternative air service. While the Islanders should be in no doubt of the strength of the Government's commitment to act only in accordance with their wishes, they should be under no illusion on the difficulties ahead or on the limits on their ability to mitigate the consequences. Unless there was a negotiated settlement, the way forward for the Islanders could only be downhill.

Further Argentine proposals

126. On 27 January 1982 the Argentine Ministry of Foreign Affairs delivered to the British Ambassador in Buenos Aires a communication in the form of a *bout de papier* setting out at length the Argentine position on its claim to sovereignty. It stated that British recognition of Argentine sovereignty over the Malvinas, South Georgia and the South Sandwich Islands remained a *sine qua non* requirement for the solution of the dispute. However much time might pass, Argentina would never abandon its claim nor relax its determination. It called for serious and in-depth negotiations culminating " within a reasonable period of time and without procrastination " in the recognition of Argentine sovereignty over the disputed Islands. It pointed out that so far there had been no concrete progress and the matter had now reached a point which " demands solutions, without further delays or dilatory arguments ". It drew attention to the fact that the United Nations Resolutions referred to the " interests " (rather

than the wishes) of the Islanders and reaffirmed Argentina's intention of respecting those interests, including the preservation of the way of life and cultural traditions of the Islanders. It claimed that the United Nations Resolutions did not refer to the " wishes " of the Islanders because the dispute was confined to the Argentine and British Governments. It also referred to the need to exploit the natural resources of the area, but stressed that " any idea of making progress in the search for pragmatic formulae for exploration and exploitation which might mean a delay or paralysis of the solution to the sovereignty question is totally unacceptable to Argentina ". In order to resolve the dispute " peacefully, definitively and *rapidly* ", Argentina proposed the establishment of a permanent negotiating commission, to meet in the first weeks of each month alternately in each capital. The commission would have a duration of one year and would be open to denunciation by either side at any time without prior warning to the other side.

127. The *bout de papier* was analysed in detail in the Foreign and Commonwealth Office. Although toughly worded, little of the substance of the paper was regarded as new. The greater part of it was seen to be a re-working of the *communiqué* issued in July 1981 (see paragraph 97). The new element was the proposal for a permanent negotiating commission working to a timetable of one year. A note, approved by Ministers, was sent to the British Ambassador in Buenos Aires as the basis on which he should speak to the Argentine Deputy Foreign Minister, Sr. Ros. The note reaffirmed that the British Government were in no doubt about British sovereignty over the Falkland Islands and their Dependencies, maritime zones and continental shelves. They could not therefore accept the Argentine assumption that the purpose of the negotiations was the eventual recognition by the British Government of Argentine sovereignty in the area. They would, however, remain ready to continue the negotiating process at the talks to be held in New York later in the month, and would be ready to discuss in detail the proposal to establish working groups to look at particular aspects of the dispute. The note also reaffirmed the British Government's wish to find, by negotiation, " an early and peaceful solution to this dispute which can be accepted by all concerned, namely the British and Argentine Governments and the people of the Falkland Islands ". The British Ambassador in Buenos Aires delivered this message on 8 February 1982.

128. In a letter on 3 February 1982, the British Ambassador in Buenos Aires reported to the Foreign and Commonwealth Office that all the indications were that Admiral Anaya, probably with President Galtieri's full agreement, had " got into the driving seat " in regard to the Malvinas negotiations and had ruled, in effect, that a test period should be allowed to see if negotiation got anywhere. The Ambassador suspected that the period allowed might be up to the 150th anniversary, in January 1983, of the British occupation of the Islands. He expected that the position of Sr. Ros, the leader of the Argentine delegation at the talks, would be very circumscribed.

Argentine press comment

129. The period leading up to the New York talks was marked by widespread comment in the Argentine press. In an article in *La Prensa* on 24 January 1982 (before the *bout de papier* was delivered), Sr. Iglesias

Rouco, a journalist regarded as usually well informed, predicted that the Argentine Government would shortly present the British Government with a series of conditions for the continuation of negotiations over the Malvinas and that, if they were not accepted, Argentina would immediately break off negotiations. He said that, according to reliable diplomatic sources, the conditions would be " firm and clear " and would set very precise time-limits for the solution of the different aspects of the problem and the final return of the Islands to Argentina. He linked this new initiative with development of Argentine policy towards the Beagle Channel, as part of " an ambitious diplomatic and strategic plan which would assure the country of a relevant role in the South Atlantic ". Sr. Rouco speculated that Argentina would receive support from the United States for any action leading to the recovery of the Islands, not excluding military action. According to the article, it was believed in both the United States and in Europe that, if the Argentine attempt to clarify the negotiations with London failed, Argentina would recover the Islands by force " this year . . . a military attempt to resolve the dispute cannot be ruled out when sovereignty is at stake ". In a further article in *La Prensa* on 7 February 1982 Sr. Rouco again predicted that the Argentine Foreign Ministry would present a series of deadlines to resolve the various aspects of the problem and a demand for British recognition of Argentine sovereignty over the Islands and of their intention to return them in accordance with United Nations resolutions. He believed that Buenos Aires was not prepared to go on talking indefinitely and that, if the British Government did not agree to bind themselves to a written timetable, would " apparently reserve the right to take other action, which might by no means exclude the recovery of the Islands by military means ".

130. On 9 February 1982 an editorial in the English language *Buenos Aires Herald* drew attention to the apparent willingness of the new Argentine Government to accept the risks any serious attempts to recover the Falkland and the Beagle Channel Islands might entail, and to hints that their Falklands/Malvinas approach would be far tougher than anything seen so far. It referred to talk of the pros and cons of simply invading the Islands and telling the world that justice had been belatedly done, but judged that invasion would be " utterly unnecessary ". However, unless the dispute was solved in the only reasonable way, by transferring the Islands to Argentina, it would be solved " in a messy and damaging way ".

131. In a further article on 18 February 1982, Sr. Rouco argued that there were three relatively new circumstances which justified taking a military initiative to recover the Malvinas: Argentina's isolation from western strategic policy; the unfavourable results of the Beagle Channel arbitration and Papal mediation; and Soviet penetration of the area. In discussion with British Embassy staff in Buenos Aires, reported by them on 19 February 1982, Sr. Rouco insisted that the opinions expressed in his articles were his own. The British Embassy was sceptical of this assertion, and subsequent intelligence, which became available at the end of February and during March 1982, indicated that the articles by Sr. Rouco, who had close connections with the Argentine Foreign Ministry and the Navy, together with other press reports, were part of a concerted effort to exert pressure on the British before the New York talks.

132. There were also articles in other journals. A long article in the magazine *Siete Dias* on 3 February 1982 reported that "unimpeachable sources" indicated that Argentina would adopt a new diplomatic approach in the next round of talks. It considered that the new impetus which the Argentine Foreign Ministry had given to foreign policy, among other things, pointed to 1982 as being the key year for the effective recovery of the Islands. Those advocating a military operation saw occupation as a consequence of British intransigence or indifference in the face of a possible Argentine ultimatum to reach a realistic understanding through peaceful negotiations. In the event of an eventual breakdown of the talks "a veritable avalanche of massive and authoritative public opinion would descend in favour of the alternative of force". It considered that, although substantive progress had not so far been achieved, Argentina would persist with "her traditional peaceful negotiating approach, perhaps in the hope that this time the United Kingdom, faced with the real alternative of armed occupation, would take the bull by the horns and press the negotiations to a final conclusion".

The New York talks

133. On 15 February 1982, in advance of the talks in New York on 26 and 27 February 1982, Lord Carrington sent a minute to the Prime Minister and to other members of the Defence Committee referring to the *bout de papier* and the proposal for a permanent negotiating commission; and to the response that the British Ambassador in Buenos Aires had been instructed to give. Lord Carrington observed that in principle the idea of setting up working groups to look at particular aspects of the dispute had considerable appeal since it was in the Government's interest to keep a dialogue going in order to avoid the difficult and costly consequences of a breakdown. But it would be necessary to resist the unrealistic timetable of work proposed by Argentina. It would also be difficult to carry the Islanders since they would be most reluctant to agree to any discussion of sovereignty with the Argentines, and the Argentines would accept nothing less. The British delegation would make it clear at the outset of the talks that any agreement reached on the future of the negotiations would be strictly *ad referendum*, but the tougher attitude being shown by the new Argentine Government, together with the strong disinclination of the Islanders to envisage any change from the *status quo*, narrowed the options. In the same minute Lord Carrington said that he expected that there would need to be a further discussion of the Falklands in the Defence Committee in March. The Prime Minister commented that it must be made clear to the Argentines that the wishes of the Islanders were paramount.

134. On 23 February 1982 Lord Buxton, the Chairman of Anglia Television, who has wide experience of matters concerning the South Atlantic, had a private conversation with Dr. Costa Mendez when he was in Buenos Aires awaiting passage on *HMS Endurance*. He gave an account of it to the British Embassy in Buenos Aires afterwards and subsequently sent Mr. Luce, on 26 March 1982, a detailed account of his interview. The British Embassy reported that Dr. Costa Mendez had stressed that sovereignty was crucial for Argentina and some alternative solution to leaseback had to be found; but he had discounted the possibility of invasion. In his later and fuller report Lord Buxton recorded that Dr. Costa Mendez

had repeatedly said that he was under pressure from public opinion, but Lord Buxton's impression had been that the pressure was coming from the Junta. Dr. Costa Mendez said he was willing to renew discussion of leaseback, provided it was presented in a different way. Lord Buxton said that he had received the clear impression that an invasion was unlikely, but that the military might plan unopposed landings, probably in South Georgia; and Dr. Costa Mendez had said that incidents such as 'Operation Condor' could not necessarily be prevented.

135. At the talks in New York at the end of February, after each side had set out its position, the British delegation presented a working paper on how it saw the framework within which a permanent negotiating commission would operate. Most of the subsequent discussion was concerned with the detailed arrangements for the commission, but the Argentine delegation pressed for a substantive response to its proposals within a month and for the commission to meet for the first time on 1 April 1982. The talks concluded with agreement of an informal working paper setting out the purpose of the permanent negotiating commission, and of a brief joint *communiqué*.

136. The purpose of the commission was stated in the working paper to be to accelerate progress towards a peaceful and comprehensive solution of the dispute. It would be presided over by Ministers, who would direct its work and decide on the agenda of, and participation in, meetings. The working paper recognised that the British delegation might include Islanders. The commission's task would be to identify all the elements in the dispute, to consider them in depth and to recommend how they might be resolved within an overall settlement. The period of operation of the commission would be for one year, at the end of which Ministers would review progress and reach conclusions on whether the commission should continue its work. During this period it would be open to either party to propose at any stage the commission's termination. Meetings would be held alternately in the capitals of the two countries, and would be chaired by the Minister of the host Government, although this function could be delegated to a senior official. The work of the commission would be conducted without prejudice to the sovereignty position of either Government. The working paper made no reference to the frequency of meetings.

137. By agreement, the joint *communiqué*, which was issued on 1 March 1982, gave none of the details of the informal working paper: its substance was confined to the following:

"The meeting took place in a cordial and positive spirit. The two sides reaffirmed their resolve to find a solution to the sovereignty dispute and considered in detail an Argentine proposal for procedures to make better progress in this sense. They agreed to inform their Governments accordingly."

Aftermath of the New York talks
Argentine action following the New York talks

138. On the day that the joint *communiqué* was issued, before the Argentine delegation had returned to Buenos Aires, the Argentine Ministry of Foreign Affairs issued a unilateral *communiqué* which, contrary to what

had been agreed in New York, disclosed the full scope of the discussions. It stated:

> "At the meeting held in New York on 26 and 27 February, the representatives of Argentina and Great Britain considered an Argentine proposal to establish a system of monthly meetings with a pre-established agenda, pre-arranged meeting place, and led by top-level officials. The aim of such meetings will be genuinely to speed up to the maximum the negotiations in train to achieve recognition of Argentine sovereignty over the Malvinas, South Georgia and the South Sandwich Islands, and by this means to achieve substantial results within a time which at this advanced stage of the discussions will necessarily have to be short.

> "Argentina has negotiated with Great Britain over the solution of the sovereignty dispute over the Islands with patience, loyalty and good faith for over 15 years, within the framework indicated by the relevant United Nations Resolutions. The new system constitutes an effective step for the early solution of the dispute. However, should this not occur, Argentina reserves to terminate the working of this mechanism and to choose freely the procedure which best accords with her interests."

139. This *communiqué* was accompanied by a good deal of press comment in Argentina. *La Nacion* quoted a Government source as saying that parallel plans had been formulated in case the proposed meetings did not produce sufficient progress towards a solution. These included recourse to the United Nations and the breaking off of economic and political relations. The source preferred, however, "at the moment" to discount suggestions of Argentina's using force to resolve the dispute. *La Prensa* speculated, after conversation with Ministry of Foreign Affairs officials, that, if present tactics were unproductive, a first step might be to cut off services to the Islands followed by a progressive cooling of bilateral relations. Sr. Rouco quoted sources saying that Britain would have no more than three or four months to acknowledge Argentine sovereignty and agree on an early date for the return of the Islands to Argentina. There would be no flexibility in Argentina's minimum demand for restitution of sovereignty before the 150th anniversary and for the holding of monthly meetings to discuss the handing over of sovereignty and guarantees for the Islanders. Thereafter Argentina would resort to other means if there was no progress. Sr. Rouco also discussed the advantages of a direct seizure of the Islands, which he believed would be "understood" by the United States, to whom joint naval facilities in the Islands could be offered. He suggested that such direct action might be taken between the middle and end of the year. The *Buenos Aires Herald* saw the Argentine statement as containing a "veiled threat" and warned Britain that this time Argentina seemed to "mean business". In its view there was no alternative to a British handover.

140. On 3 March Mr. Luce sent a personal message to Sr. Ros expressing concern about the unilateral *communiqué*, which contravened the understanding in New York that the proposals would remain confidential until Governments had been consulted. He said that the *communiqué* and accompanying press comment created a more difficult and unhelpful climate for continuing the negotiating process. Mr. Luce added that he was deeply disturbed by what might be interpreted as threats and that it would

be very difficult to make progress unless there was a clear understanding that the issue could only be resolved through peaceful negotiation.

141. On 4 March the British Ambassador in Buenos Aires saw Sr. Ros, who assured him that he had been unaware of the unilateral *communiqué* and accepted that it was unfortunate. He also said that the Ministry of Foreign Affairs accepted no responsibility for remarks ascribed to it unattributably in the press. The British Ambassador saw Dr. Costa Mendez the following day, who explained formally and at some length Argentine dissatisfaction with progress, but denied that the Argentine Government wished in any way to threaten. Dr. Costa Mendez referred to statements he had made earlier that day in Brazil making it clear that the Argentine Government were not imposing deadlines but setting out a proposed programme which included only recourses contemplated in the United Nations Charter. He repeated the need for a programme of monthly meetings.

Mr. Enders's visit to Buenos Aires

142. Following the New York talks Mr. Luce went to Washington to see Mr. Thomas Enders, the United States Assistant Secretary of State for Latin American Affairs, before Mr. Enders's forthcoming official visit to Buenos Aires. Mr. Luce briefed Mr. Enders on the British Government's position on the dispute and the progress of negotiations. In view of the danger of confrontation if negotiations broke down, Mr. Luce asked him to encourage the Argentines to "keep things cool", which Mr. Enders undertook to do.

143. Following the unilateral *communiqué* on 1 March 1982 the British Ambassador in Washington was also asked to brief Mr. Enders on the terms of the British reaction and make it clear that, while the British Government had every wish to find a solution to the dispute, it was politically impossible to negotiate against a background of threats. There was not time, however, for this to be done before Mr. Enders left for Buenos Aires, and instead the British Ambassador in Buenos Aires was asked to brief the United States Embassy there in similar terms.

144. Mr. Enders visited Buenos Aires from Sunday 6 to Tuesday 8 March 1982, and met, among others, President Galtieri and Dr. Costa Mendez. *La Prensa* reported that he had been given a very full report on the progress of the Falklands negotiations. The British Ambassador in Buenos Aires reported that his information from the American Embassy was that Mr. Enders had not taken the opportunity specifically to advise the Argentines to keep the temperature down, but Mr. Enders himself subsequently asked that Mr. Luce be informed that he had raised the matter both privately with Dr. Costa Mendez and publicly, stressing the strategic and human aspects of the problem, both of which had to be resolved for a successful outcome. Although the Argentines had been somewhat non-committal, they had not given him the impression that they were about to do anything drastic.

A Uruguayan view

145. On 3 March the British Ambassador in Montevideo reported to the British Ambassador in Buenos Aires, and to the Foreign and Commonwealth Office, the views of a leading Uruguayan, who had told her that he had

been struck by the much tougher way in which everyone in Buenos Aires was talking about the Falkland Islands. He thought that, if Argentina did not get what it wanted, it might well take some military action.

The Foreign and Commonwealth Office's assessment of the situation

146. On his return to London Mr. Luce answered a Parliamentary Question on 3 March([1]) on the discussions he had held in New York. In answer to supplementary questions he stated that there would be no contemplation of any transfer of sovereignty without consulting the wishes of the Islanders, or without the consent of the House. He referred to the *communiqué* issued by the Argentine Ministry of Foreign Affairs as " not helpful to the process that we all wish to see, that will resolve this dispute "; and, when asked for an assurance that all necessary steps were in hand to ensure the protection of the Islands against unexpected attack, said, " we have no doubts about our sovereignty over the Falkland Islands and no doubt about our duties to the Islanders ".

147. At a short meeting on 5 March 1982 Lord Carrington reviewed the situation with Mr. Luce, Mr. Ure and Mr. Fearn. In accordance with normal Foreign and Commonwealth Office practice, no minutes of the meeting were taken, but Mr. Ure recorded the points for action that had emerged. These were that:

(i) draft messages should be prepared urgently for Mr. Luce to send to Sr. Ros, and for Lord Carrington to send to Dr. Costa Mendez urging him to put the talks back on the rails on the lines agreed in New York;

(ii) a draft personal message should be prepared for Lord Carrington to send to Mr. Haig;

(iii) a note should be prepared on United Nations Resolutions on the Falklands; and the Department should consider what initiative might be taken there if the present negotiations broke down; and

(iv) a draft paper should be prepared for a Defence Committee meeting to be held " fairly soon ", probably as soon as the Argentine response to the ministerial messages was received.

Mr. Ure recorded that the Cabinet Office had said that the Prime Minister would like the next Defence Committee paper on the Falklands to include annexes on both civil and military contingency plans.

148. Although the fact is not recorded in Mr. Ure's note, he also took the opportunity, after consulting the Permanent Under-Secretary of State (who was not present at the meeting) to tell Lord Carrington that, in November 1977, at an earlier period of heightened tension in the dispute, the previous Government had covertly sent a small naval task force to the area. Lord Carrington asked whether the Argentines had known about it and, when told that they had not, he did not pursue the matter. Officials did not recommend to Ministers at the meeting that they should consider a similar naval deployment.

Intelligence reports

149. In early March 1982 a number of intelligence reports were available indicating the views of Argentine Ministers and officials in the preceding

---

([1]) *Official Report*, House of Commons, 3 March 1982, Cols. 263–264.

43

3145006   G*

weeks. The general tenor of these reports was that, while it was important for the Argentine Government to make progress in the negotiations, military action was not being contemplated in the immediate future. Reports available immediately prior to the New York talks reflected the views of Argentine officials that there would be no invasion unless the talks broke down; that it would be unrealistic to think of invasion before the next southern summer; and that invasion was not considered a realistic option. A further report at the beginning of March, reflecting an Argentine diplomatic view, was to the effect that Argentina was determined to achieve progress on sovereignty by the end of the year; and, if this was not forthcoming, would take the issue to the General Assembly with a view to obtaining a declaration recognising Argentine sovereignty over the Falklands. There was information that Dr. Costa Mendez had decided that, if the talks did not produce results, a campaign would be mounted against Britain in international organisations; if this failed and the talks on the Beagle Channel made no progress, there was likely to be little alternative to the use of force.

150. On 2 March 1982 the British Defence *Attaché* in Buenos Aires wrote to the Governor of the Falkland Islands, copying his letter to the Ministry of Defence and the Foreign and Commonwealth Office (where it was received on about 9 March) on the Argentine military threat to the Falklands. This followed a private visit that he had made to the Islands on his own initiative in January 1982 to enable him to judge at first hand the military situation there in the event of Argentine action. On his return to Buenos Aires he had briefed the British Ambassador there about his visit, but had not made a formal report in view of its unofficial nature. In the light of later developments, in particular Argentine press comment about the possibility of military measures, the Defence *Attaché* decided to circulate his views more widely. In his letter he commented that, on the worst possible interpretation of developments, an Army President, who had already demonstrated his lack of patience when frustrated over such issues, could give orders to the military to solve the Malvinas problem once and for all in the latter half of the year. He judged that, unless and until the talks broke down, the most likely threat was posed by the Argentine Navy, which could take a number of measures to demonstrate how the Argentine claim to sovereignty could be backed by strength, such as establishing a naval presence on an outlying island or landing marines on one of the islands for a twenty-four hour exercise. If the Argentines came to believe that a negotiated settlement was no longer possible, a straight seizure of the Islands was an obvious alternative. The Defence *Attaché* pointed out that in Argentina a military *coup* was a fairly well practised art; the Argentine Army studied and admired *coup de main* operations of all sorts. He examined several ways in which Argentina might mount an operation of this kind, and pointed out that the chance of providing early warning from Argentina could be increased if some special arrangements could be made, but that as things were they could not realistically expect to be able to detect any Argentine military moves.

151. On 10 March an officer in the Defence Intelligence Staff of the Ministry of Defence circulated a minute widely within the Ministry of Defence; it was also copied to the Foreign and Commonwealth Office. It drew attention to recent intelligence indicating that the belligerent press comment had been inspired by the Argentine Navy in an attempt to achieve

an early settlement of the dispute. The intelligence also indicated that, if there was no tangible progress towards a settlement by the end of June, the Argentine Navy would push for a diplomatic offensive in international organisations, a break in relations with Britain and military action against the Islands, but that neither President Galtieri nor the Army was thinking along those lines. Summarising the position, the minute said that all other diplomatic and intelligence reporting in recent weeks confirmed that all elements of the Argentine Government apart from the Navy favoured diplomatic action to solve the dispute and that the military option was not under active consideration at that time. It saw no reason to believe that the Argentine Navy had any prospect of persuading the President or other Government members to adopt its proposed course of action or of going it alone; and did not therefore consider that the Navy's attitude posed any immediate or increased threat to the Falkland Islands beyond that outlined in the most recent Joint Intelligence Committee assessment, prepared in July 1981.

The Prime Minister's reaction to the deteriorating diplomatic situation

152. On 3 March the British Ambassador in Buenos Aires had reported further comment in the Argentine press on the unilateral *communiqué* (see paragraph 139). When the Prime Minister saw this telegram, she wrote on it, " we must make contingency plans ". Her Private Secretary wrote to the Foreign and Commonwealth Office on 8 March, copying his letter to the Ministry of Defence and the Cabinet Office, recording the Prime Minister's comment and saying that he understood that it might be the intention of Lord Carrington to bring a further paper on the Falkland Islands to the Defence Committee in the fairly near future; and that the Foreign and Commonwealth Office might think that this could helpfully contain an account of contingency planning. No immediate response was made to the letter because, we believe, of the general expectation in Whitehall that it would be included on the agenda of an early meeting of the Defence Committee.

153. On 8 March the Prime Minister also spoke to Mr. Nott and asked him how quickly Royal Naval ships could be deployed to the Falkland Islands, if required. The Ministry of Defence replied on 12 March indicating which ships were then deployed in the West Indies, and on exercise in the Gulf of Mexico and off the eastern seaboard of the United States. The reply pointed out that passage time for a frigate deployed to the Falklands, which would require Royal Fleet Auxiliary support, would be in the order of 20 days.

Diplomatic initiatives

154. On further consideration of the action agreed at Lord Carrington's meeting on 5 March 1982 (see paragraph 147), it was decided to send only one message to the Argentine Government, from Lord Carrington to Dr. Costa Mendez. A draft was sent to the Governor on 8 March for considera- tion by the Island Councillors. It expressed Lord Carrington's pleasure at the progress that had been made in New York towards setting up new procedures for carrying forward and giving fresh impetus to negotiations about the future of the Islands, which reflected the Government's determina- tion to achieve a peaceful solution to a difficult issue which would be acceptable to both Governments and to the people of the Falkland Islands,

45

while expressing disappointment at the statements which had been made in the press reports in Buenos Aires following the talks. It sought agreement on " two essential points ": first, that the negotiating commission would encompass all aspects of possible approaches to a solution of the dispute, without prejudice to either side's position on sovereignty; and, secondly, that the negotiations could not be pursued against a background of threats from either side of retaliatory action if they broke down. At a joint meeting of the Island Councils on 16 March, which had been brought forward from 18 March for this purpose, there was unanimous support for the message as drafted. The Councillors asked the Governor to emphasise that there could be no negotiations on the *transfer of sovereignty;* their aim would be to convince Argentina that Britain had the stronger claim to the Islands and that the Islanders were determined to stay British.

155. On 18 March a draft telegram to the British Ambassador in Buenos Aires was submitted to Mr. Luce and Lord Carrington incorporating the message to Dr. Costa Mendez. Officials were not optimistic that Argentina would accept the message as a basis for future negotiations. They took the view that it would be necessary to work on the assumption that the Argentine reply would be negative and that Argentina might resort at an early stage to retaliatory measures. This view was reinforced by recent intelligence indicating that, unless a satisfactory reply meeting Argentine conditions was received by the end of March 1982 at the latest, early action to withdraw Argentine services to the Islands might be taken. Officials recommended that, in advance of the proposed discussion in the Defence Committee, Lord Carrington should seek Mr. Nott's agreement, on a contingency basis, to maintain *HMS Endurance* on station in the area for the time being; and should circulate to members of the Defence Committee the paper by officials seeking political and financial authority to carry forward urgently contingency plans for the replacement of services to the Islands. This paper was submitted to Foreign and Commonwealth Office Ministers on 19 March 1982.

156. Lord Carrington subsequently decided to circulate the draft of the proposed reply to Dr. Costa Mendez to his colleagues with his minute of 24 March 1982 (see paragraph 187) to the Prime Minister, but it was held up in consequence of events on South Georgia and was never sent.

157. The second initiative decided on at Lord Carrington's meeting on 5 March was the sending of a personal message to Mr. Haig. This was sent to the British Embassy in Washington on 8 March for delivery to Mr. Haig. It expressed the British Government's increasing concern about the Argentine Government's attitude, in particular about the threats in the Argentine press, apparently with some measure of Government inspiration, to use force if the negotiations did not soon reach a conclusion on Argentine terms. It said that Mr. Haig would realise that it was politically impossible to negotiate against such a background, so that anything that Mr. Enders could do while in Buenos Aires to bring the Argentines to a more reasonable and pacific frame of mind would be much appreciated: it was in everyone's interest that the issue should not be allowed to develop into a dangerous source of tension in the region. Lord Carrington expressed the hope that the Government could count on Mr.

Haig's help in ensuring that the issue was settled peacefully and in accordance with the democratically expressed wishes of the inhabitants of the Islands. Mr. Haig's reply was delivered on 15 March. In it he referred to Mr. Enders's visit to Buenos Aires, where he had urged the Argentines to continue negotiations. He said that they had been non-committal but not negative. Mr. Haig added that, as opportunities presented themselves, the Americans would continue to urge a constructive approach with due regard for all interests at stake.

Intelligence : mid-March 1982

158. In mid-March Foreign and Commonwealth Office Ministers received a number of intelligence reports. One reported that Mr. Enders had been told during his visit that Argentina planned to mount an international diplomatic offensive if there were no immediate signs of British willingness to bring negotiations to a successful conclusion within the next year; the report claimed that Mr. Enders had indicated that the United States Government would see no problem in this course of action. Another, reflecting Argentine military views, referred to a plan to achieve gradual British withdrawal from the Falklands over a period of 30 years, at the end of which full sovereignty would pass to Argentina; the talk of invasion since the New York negotiations was said to have been part of a design to put psychological pressure on Britain. A further report indicated that senior Argentine naval officers doubted that Argentina would invade the Falklands, although it would be relatively simple to do so and they thought that Britain would not prevent it.

159. Other intelligence reports indicated that the Junta had been displeased with the agreement reached in New York and that the unilateral Ministry of Foreign Affairs *communiqué* had been issued on the orders of the President. The view of the Ministry of Foreign Affairs was said to be that the negotiating team in New York had properly carried out its instructions except in failing to obtain British agreement to a date in March 1982 for a meeting to begin the monthly series of talks. This had caused the trouble with the Government. It had been decided that, if no reply were forthcoming from the British side on a date in March 1982, Argentina would retaliate by withdrawing the air or sea services to the Islands. There had been no final decision on the action to be taken if the British agreed to a date after March but there was a disposition in the Ministry of Foreign Affairs to take action to show all concerned that they were serious. Dr. Costa Mendez was also concerned to make up for the Argentine failure in the Beagle Channel dispute. An invasion was said not to have been seriously considered but in the last resort it could not be discounted in view of the unpredictability of the President and some senior members of the armed forces.

160. At this stage in the diplomatic exchanges with Argentina, the initiatives directed towards the resumption of negotiations on the basis agreed at the New York talks at the end of February were, in effect, overtaken by the South Georgia incident, with which we deal in Chapter 3.

19 MARCH–2 APRIL 1982

The South Georgia incident

Sr. Davidoff's contract and visit to South Georgia in December 1981

161. Sr. Constantino Davidoff, a scrap metal merchant from Buenos Aires, first approached Christian Salvesen, the Edinburgh-based firm managing the Crown leases for the disused whaling stations on South Georgia, in 1978. The following year he signed a contract giving him an option to purchase equipment and dispose of it. The option was exercised in 1980 under an agreement that any equipment remaining after March 1983 would revert to Salvesens. Sr. Davidoff was occasionally in contact with the British Embassy in Buenos Aires in 1980 and 1981.

162. Sr. Davidoff left Buenos Aires on 16 December 1981 on the Argentine naval ice-breaker, *Almirante Irizar,* to inspect the scrap on South Georgia and arrived at Leith on 20 December. He notified the British Embassy in Buenos Aires of the visit in a letter which arrived after he had departed.

163. On 31 December 1981 the Governor of the Falkland Islands relayed to the Foreign and Commonwealth Office a report by the British Antarctic Survey Base Commander at Grytviken of the unauthorised presence of the *Almirante Irizar* in Stromness Bay. The Governor pointed out that the *Almirante Irizar* was required by the Dependencies' legislation to obtain entry clearance at Grytviken and that Sr. Davidoff knew this. He recommended instituting proceedings against Sr. Davidoff and making a strong protest to the Argentine Government.

164. A reply was sent instructing the Governor not to institute proceedings, which "would risk provoking a most serious incident which could escalate and have an unforeseeable outcome". He was instructed that, if Sr. Davidoff presented himself at Grytviken and asked for entry clearance, it should be granted; if the Argentine vessel was naval and clearance for her also was not sought, the Base Commander should deliver a formal written protest; if Sr. Davidoff attempted to land at Grytviken without proper clearance, the party should be ordered to depart immediately but without threats being used; and, if it refused to comply, further instructions should be sought from the Foreign and Commonwealth Office. The reply also said that the Foreign and Commonwealth Office would probably wish in due course to make a protest to the Argentine Government but would first see what transpired at Grytviken.

165. On 4 January 1982 the Foreign and Commonwealth Office instructed the Ambassador in Buenos Aires to deliver a formal protest in the strongest terms at this violation of British sovereignty and warn against the undesirable consequences which could follow from a repetition. The Ambassador was to say that, if any further attempt were made to land at Grytviken or elsewhere in South Georgia without proper authority, the British Government reserved the right to take whatever action might be necessary, and that it was up to Sr. Davidoff to comply with the laws of the Falkland Islands Dependencies. The British Ambassador in Buenos Aires approached the Argentine Ministry of Foreign Affairs on 6 January,

but withheld the protest pending an investigation by the Ministry, which denied any knowledge of the incident. Following the receipt of evidence corroborating the visit of the *Almirante Irizar,* the Foreign and Commonwealth Office instructed the British Embassy on 3 February 1982 to lodge a formal protest. The Embassy reported on 9 February that the protest had been delivered, and on 18 February that the Argentine Ministry of Foreign Affairs had rejected it.

HMS Endurance's *reception in Argentine ports*

166. On 8 January 1982 Captain Barker, the Captain of *HMS Endurance,* reported that he had spoken by radio to Captain Trombetta, the Officer commanding the Argentine Antarctic Squadron, who was embarked on the *Almirante Irizar.* Captain Trombetta had told him that he was *en route* for the Belgrano base in the Antarctic, but shortly afterwards it had become apparent that he was really making for Southern Thule. Later in the month, on 25 January 1982, Captain Barker reported that *HMS Endurance* had received a cold reception at the Argentine port of Ushuaia. He had heard that there had been an order not to fraternise with the British. An Argentine pilot had told him on his departure that something was "very wrong" with the Argentine Navy. In contrast to her reception at Ushuaia, *HMS Endurance* was warmly received when she visited another Argentine port, Mar del Plata, shortly afterwards.

The landing on South Georgia on 19 March 1982

167. The British Ambassador in Buenos Aires reported on 23 February 1982 that Sr. Davidoff had called at the Embassy that morning. He had apologised for the problems caused by his visit on the *Almirante Irizar* in December 1981 and said that he intended soon to return to South Georgia with a party to salvage the equipment. He was anxious not to create difficulties and had asked for full instructions on how to proceed. The Ambassador sought advice from the Governor on this point, but did not receive a substantive reply before the party left for South Georgia.

168. On 9 March Sr. Davidoff sent the British Embassy in Buenos Aires formal notification that 41 workmen were going to South Georgia on 11 March on the *Bahia Buen Suceso,* an Argentine naval support vessel, and would remain there for an initial period of four months. He offered to transport supplies to the British Antarctic Survey and to make available to them the services of a doctor and nurse travelling with the party. The British Embassy reported this to the Governor and informed the Foreign and Commonwealth Office, and asked Sr. Davidoff for further details of the ship and the workmen. Salvesens reported to the Foreign and Commonwealth Office and to the Governor on 16 March that Sr. Davidoff had notified them of the visit and that they had granted his request for an extension of the contract to 31 March 1984.

169. On 20 March the Governor of the Falkland Islands informed the Foreign and Commonwealth Office of a signal from the Base Commander at Grytviken late the previous day. The British Antarctic Survey had observed the *Bahia Buen Suceso* in Leith Harbour and a sizeable party of civilian and military personnel ashore. Shots had been heard, the Argentine flag had been raised, and a notice warning against unauthorised landings had been defaced. The British Antarctic Survey had informed the Argentines

that they should have reported to Grytviken, but was told that permission had been given by the British Embassy in Buenos Aires. The Governor instructed the Base Commander to tell the Argentines again to report to Grytviken and to lower the Argentine flag. The Governor gave his view that the Argentine Navy was using Sr. Davidoff as a front to establish an Argentine presence on South Georgia. He suggested that, since this was the second violation by Sr. Davidoff, the party should be ordered to leave even if it did report to Grytviken. Having consulted Captain Barker, he also suggested that *HMS Endurance* should sail to South Georgia with marines to enforce the eviction. The Foreign and Commonwealth Office approved the instructions to the Base Commander at Grytviken, but said that Ministers would need to be consulted about the deployment of *HMS Endurance*. The Foreign and Commonwealth Office instructed the British Embassy in Buenos Aires to give a message to the Argentine Ministry of Foreign Affairs that the incident was regarded as serious and that, if the *Bahia Buen Suceso* did not leave forthwith, the British Government would have to take whatever action seemed necessary. The message also indicated that, while both sides were considering how best to continue negotiations on the sovereignty dispute in order to solve it peacefully, it would be hard to understand if the Argentine Government endorsed the incident. The Argentine *Chargé d'Affaires* in London was also summoned and given this message. The British Ambassador in Buenos Aires reported that the Ministry of Foreign Affairs professed to have been unaware of the visit. He confirmed that Sr. Davidoff had not been given any permission by the British Embassy. He advised that great restraint should be used, at least until it was clear whether or not the incident was a deliberate challenge authorised at high level. Foreign and Commonwealth Office and Defence Ministers agreed the *HMS Endurance* should sail for South Georgia the next day, with additional marines, unless the Argentines obeyed the Governor's instructions. The Commander-in-Chief, Fleet, sent the necessary instructions to *HMS Endurance* towards midnight on 20 March 1982. The Governor was instructed to report any developments on South Georgia and to keep the destination of *HMS Endurance* confidential, in order to avoid the appearance of escalating the incident.

170. The following day, Sunday 21 March, the Base Commander at Grytviken, who had arranged an observation party at Leith, reported that the Argentine flag had been lowered, but that there was no indication that the Argentines were preparing to leave. The British Ambassador in Buenos Aires reported the Argentine Government's official response, which, without making an apology, expressed the hope that the significance of the affair would not be exaggerated. It confirmed that the party and the ship would be leaving the same day; that they were in no way official; and that the party included no serving service personnel and was not carrying military arms. The Foreign and Commonwealth Office informed the Governor that *HMS Endurance* would sail for South Georgia unless the Argentine ship and party left, and asked for confirmation that the party was civilian. The Base Commander reported that some of the Argentines were dressed in what appeared to him to be military-style clothing and had behaved in a military way, but had not carried firearms. Between 50 and 60 Argentines had been seen, most of them in civilian clothing. Although no firearms had been seen, further shots had been heard and reindeer had been killed, which was contrary to the provisions of Sr. Davidoff's contract.

171. On Monday 22 March the Base Commander at Grytviken reported that the *Bahia Buen Suceso* had sailed from Leith and that there was no sign of the shore party.

172. On the same day the Governor telegraphed a personal message to Lord Carrington from Lord Buxton, who said that he had gained the impression from his recent talk with Dr. Costa Mendez (see paragraph 134) that open attack was unlikely but that casual unopposed landings were probable. He urged that Sr. Davidoff should not be regarded as a casual scrap-dealer and that his contract should be rescinded immediately in view of the deliberate breaches of its terms. He judged that, if the British reaction was placatory, more illegal landings would follow, the next time probably on the Falkland Islands.

173. The Argentine *Chargé d'Affaires* informed the Foreign and Commonwealth Office that the *Bahia Buen Suceso* had departed from Leith on 21 March, leaving behind equipment, and that he assumed that all the personnel had left with the ship. He stressed that the action taken by Sr. Davidoff had been on his own responsibility and in no way reflected any deliberate intention by the Argentine Government to raise the political temperature; the ship was not a warship but a naval transport vessel operating under a commercial charter and without service personnel or weapons on board. The Foreign and Commonwealth Office informed the *Chargé d'Affaires* that the British Government had no wish to build up the incident. *HMS Endurance* was instructed to resume her normal duties unless the Base Commander reported a continued Argentine pressure at Leith.

174. On 22 March diplomatic exchanges also took place in Buenos Aires, where the Ministry of Foreign Affairs expressed concern at news of an insult to the Argentine flag at the LADE (Argentine Air Force airline) office in Port Stanley. The Governor reported that on the night of 20/21 March the LADE office had been entered, apparently by someone using a key. A Union Flag had been placed over the Argentine flag there and " tit for tat, you buggers " written in toothpaste on a desk. In a later incident, during the night of 22/23 March, " UK OK " was written on two external windows of the LADE office.

175. Later on 22 March the Base Commander at Grytviken reported that some Argentines were still at Leith, and that a French yacht, the *Cinq Gars Pour,* had ignored his instructions not to go to Leith and was making contact with the Argentines. Captain Barker sent a signal expressing his view that there were indications of collusion between Sr. Davidoff and the Argentine Navy. The naval headquarters in Buenos Aires had congratulated the *Bahia Buen Suceso* on a successful operation and directed her to return to Buenos Aires as soon as possible. The Governor strongly recommended that *HMS Endurance* should be instructed to remove the men from Leith.

176. *HMS Endurance* was ordered to continue towards South Georgia and await further instructions. The same evening, the British Ambassador in Buenos Aires reported that the Ministry of Foreign Affairs had confirmed that some men had been left behind at Leith but had urged that no forceful action should be taken which would irritate public opinion in Argentina.

177. On 23 March Captain Barker sent a signal suggesting that the events in South Georgia were linked with the misinformation he had been given in January 1982 about the activities of the *Almirante Irizar* (see paragraph 166) and with three recent Argentine Air Force overflights of South Georgia. The signal also noted that the *Bahia Buen Suceso* had observed strict radio silence throughout her stay at South Georgia. In drawing this signal to the attention of Mr. Luce, Foreign and Commonwealth Office officials commented that it was evidence that the operation in South Georgia had been undertaken with the full knowledge and probable guidance of the Argentine Navy.

178. The Base Commander at Grytviken reported that there were an estimated ten Argentines left at Leith. Ministerial approval was given for *HMS Endurance* and the Royal Marines aboard her to be used to remove them.

179. That afternoon Mr. Luce made the following statement to the House of Commons:(¹)

"We were informed on 20 March by the commander of the British Antarctic survey base at Grytviken on South Georgia that a party of Argentines had landed at Leith harbour nearby. The base commander informed the Argentine party that its presence was illegal as it had not obtained his prior authority for the landing. We immediately took the matter up with the Argentine authorities in Buenos Aires and the Argentine embassy in London and, following our approach, the ship and most of the personnel left on 21 March. However, the base commander has reported that a small number of men and some equipment remain. We are therefore making arrangements to ensure their early departure."

In reply to questions expressing concern, Mr. Luce referred to the presence in the area of *HMS Endurance,* which was in a position to help if necessary. He also said that it was the duty of any British Government to defend the Islands to the best of their ability but that the deployment of a defence force was a matter for the Defence Secretary.

180. The British Ambassador in Buenos Aires was informed by the Foreign and Commonwealth Office that Ministers had decided that *HMS Endurance* should continue to South Georgia in order to remove the remaining Argentines. He was instructed to tell the Ministry of Foreign Affairs that the continued presence of the Argentines, contrary to previous assurances, left no option but to take this action, which was the regrettable result of Sr. Davidoff's own irresponsibility. The intention was to conduct the operation correctly, peacefully and in as low a key as possible.

181. On the same day (23 March) the British Ambassador in Buenos Aires reported that he had been summoned to see Sr. Ros, who had asked him to account for the incident in the LADE office at Port Stanley and sought an assurance that the matter would be investigated and any breach of the peace duly punished. Sr. Ros had also asked for co-operation to reduce the landing at Leith to more realistic proportions since the men left were simple workmen. The British Ambassador told Sr. Ros that the British Government shared his wish to avoid exaggeration.

(¹) *Official Report,* House of Commons, 23 March 1982, Col. 798.

182. Later in the day the British Ambassador was summoned to see Dr. Costa Mendez, who expressed surprise that the British Government were proceeding so rapidly to such very grave action, without exhausting the diplomatic options. Dr. Costa Mendez gave a solemn warning that, if action to remove the party on South Georgia was not postponed, those like himself and Sr. Ros who were trying to deal with the Falklands in a moderate way, would lose control of events. Harsh action would precipitate a harsh response, but he could not predict what it would be, nor could he undertake to keep it within bounds. Dr. Costa Mendez agreed to look at the British Ambassador's suggestion that the *Bahia Buen Suceso* might return to remove the men and urged that in the meantime *HMS Endurance* should not take any action. He added that the incident illustrated the need to get on with the main negotiations and suggested that it might be held over as a first subject for discussion by the negotiating commission.

183. In reporting this conversation to the Foreign and Commonwealth Office, the British Ambassador warned that, seen from Buenos Aires, the British Government's reaction to Sr. Davidoff's "trivial and low-level misbehaviour" could do lasting damage to the whole structure of bilateral relations.

184. Foreign and Commonwealth Office Ministers decided to make a further attempt to resolve the problem without provocation. *HMS Endurance* was ordered to wait at Grytviken instead of proceeding to Leith. The British Ambassador in Buenos Aires was instructed to pass on a personal message from Lord Carrington to Dr. Costa Mendez agreeing to the removal of the men by the *Bahia Buen Suceso;* but making it clear that it was essential that they should be removed without delay. Failing this, they would be removed by other means. The message also said that it was essential not to lose sight of the overriding need to ensure the right political climate for mutual efforts to resolve the Falklands dispute peacefully through negotiations.

185. In the evening of 23 March Dr. Costa Mendez told the British Ambassador in Buenos Aires that he welcomed Lord Carrington's message. He had discussed the issue with the Junta. Dr. Costa Mendez said that he assumed it would be possible for another Argentine ship to remove the men, and was about to discuss this with the military. In reporting this conversation to the Foreign and Commonwealth Office, the British Ambassador commented that he thought Dr. Costa Mendez was trying to be helpful and sensible, but he was on a short rein with public opinion and the military.

186. On 24 March the British Ambassador reported that Dr. Costa Mendez had told him that he was hopeful of arranging the removal of the men by another vessel but that the decision would be made at a meeting of the Commanders-in-Chief.

187. On the same day Lord Carrington sent a minute to the Prime Minister and other members of the Defence Committee about the Falkland Islands dispute generally. He said that, since he had last reported, on 15 February 1982, the dispute had developed to a point where an early confrontation with Argentina might need to be faced. He referred to the difficult and demanding proposal that Argentina had put forward at the

New York talks; to the subsequent Ministry of Foreign Affairs *communiqué* and bellicose press comment; and to the South Georgia incident. He circulated with his minute the draft message to Dr. Costa Mendez (prepared after his meeting on 5 March but never sent (see paragraphs 147 and 156)). The message was as follows:

"I was pleased to hear from Richard Luce about the progress which the Argentine and British delegations (with the assistance of the Falkland Islands Councillors) made in New York on 26 and 27 February towards setting up new procedures for carrying forward and giving fresh impetus to negotiations about the future of the Islands. This reflected our determination to achieve a peaceful solution to this difficult issue, which would be acceptable to your Government, to the British Government and to the people of the Falkland Islands. You must also know of our subsequent disappointment (which Richard Luce has made clear to Sr. Ros) at the statements which have been made, and the press reports which have been appearing, in Buenos Aires since the conclusion of those talks.

"I therefore think it would be helpful, if we are to be able to proceed further along the lines discussed in New York, that we should confirm our respective Governments' agreement on two essential points. Firstly, it is understood that the work of the proposed Negotiating Commission will encompass all aspects of and possible approaches to a solution of the dispute without prejudice to either side's position on sovereignty. These talks must be genuine negotiations and cannot be based on any predetermined assumptions on what the outcome might be. Secondly, these negotiations cannot be pursued against a background of threats from either side of retaliatory action if they break down. We would welcome your assurance that the Argentine Government intends to further the negotiations on this basis.

"In the spirit of the recent meeting in New York, and so that there may be no misunderstanding, I would intend, once you have replied, to publish this message and, with your permission, your reply."

188. Lord Carrington said in his minute that the draft message had been agreed by the Falkland Islands Councillors, but that it would require amendment before issue to take account of developments over the illegal landing on South Georgia. Once the Argentines replied, he intended to publish the text of his message in order to demonstrate to both British and international opinion the importance the British Government attached to achieving a solution of the dispute through peaceful and genuine negotiations. He could not, however, be confident that the message would be acceptable to the Argentines. Argentina had built up a dangerous head of steam on the issue and Argentine public opinion had been led to expect rapid progress only on Argentine terms and with the sole objective of arranging an early transfer of sovereignty. It was therefore necessary to recognise that negotiations might be at an end and that the Argentines would turn to other forms of pressure: international action at the United Nations, diplomatic and commercial reprisals, and, in the final analysis, military action against the Islands. Lord Carrington recommended an early meeting of the Defence Committee to consider the full implications and the action it might be necessary to take in response. He also sought approval for officials to carry forward civil contingency plans to replace air and sea services to the Falklands

and financial approval to meet such costs from the Contingency Reserve. The Chief Secretary to the Treasury replied to Lord Carrington on 29 March saying that he could not agree to meeting the cost from the Contingency Reserve.

189. Also on 24 March Lord Carrington wrote separately to Mr. Nott seeking agreement to *HMS Endurance's* remaining on station for the time being and suggesting that, in advance of the next Defence Committee meeting to discuss the Falklands, the Ministry of Defence should circulate a paper on military contingency planning.

190. Intelligence was also circulated indicating that Admiral Anaya, the Argentine Naval Commander-in-Chief, was behind the hardening Argentine position on South Georgia and that the Navy was planning to do something if the Argentine proposal made at the New York talks did not produce tangible progress towards the transfer of sovereignty within the next few months. It was said that Admiral Anaya had been responsible for the deliberate raising of the temperature since the beginning of the year in order to prepare public opinion; but that there was no central co-ordination of policy, which was conducted from several quarters, including the Ministry of Foreign Affairs and the Navy.

191. Late in the evening of 24 March the British Ambassador in Buenos Aires was summoned by Dr. Costa Mendez, who told him that he was having great difficulty, particularly with Admiral Anaya, in taking any action under the threat of force implied in the deployment of *HMS Endurance*. Dr. Costa Mendez said that he had been reassured to learn that *HMS Endurance* had sailed to Grytviken rather than Leith and undertook to see whether Sr. Davidoff could be persuaded to arrange for the removal of the party, perhaps on a scientific ship which was in the area, but he was doubtful whether he would succeed.

192. Also on 24 March, the British Defence *Attaché* in Buenos Aires sent the Ministry of Defence a telegram bringing up to date his earlier assessment of the Argentine military threat to the Falklands. He judged that any attempt at forcible removal of the Argentines from Leith would be met by force, either from a warship at sea or by a " rescue operation " at Port Stanley if the workmen were taken there. The latter could escalate into an occupation of the Falkland Islands. Escalation would suit the hawks in the Argentine Government, who were pressing the leadership to take advantage of the incident. The Defence *Attaché* advised that, before *HMS Endurance* was committed, it would be necessary to take into account the increase in the threat to Port Stanley.

The days leading up to the invasion

Thursday 25 March

193. On 25 March information was received in London of the despatch of Argentine warships to prevent *HMS Endurance* from evacuating the Argentines from Leith and of the deployment of further ships to intercept *HMS Endurance,* if required, between South Georgia and the Falkland Islands. Later in the day *HMS Endurance* reported that a second Argentine ship, the *Bahia Paraiso,* had arrived at Leith and was working cargo. In the evening *HMS Endurance* reported three landing craft and a military

helicopter between the *Bahia Paraiso* and the jetty at Leith. She also reported that the *Bahia Paraiso* was flying the pennant of the Argentine Navy's Senior Officer, Antarctic Squadron. At that stage the Foreign and Commonwealth Office believed that the *Bahia Paraiso,* although an Argentine naval vessel, was an unarmed, scientific ship.

194. That morning Lord Carrington reported to Cabinet on the situation in South Georgia. He said that *HMS Endurance* was then at Grytviken and could remove the remaining Argentines from Leith, but that public opinion in Argentina was in a highly charged state over the incident and there was a real risk that, if *HMS Endurance* took this action, Argentine warships in the area might either intercept *HMS Endurance* on her way back to Port Stanley, or carry out some counter-action against the Falkland Islands themselves. Efforts were therefore continuing to persuade the Argentine Government to evacuate the men. There seemed certain to be an adverse effect on negotiations over the Falkland Islands, in which event the Islands' air link might be cut. If the Argentines thereafter threatened military action, Britain would face an almost impossible task in seeking to defend the Islands at such long range. The Cabinet noted that the withdrawal from service of *HMS Endurance* might need to be reconsidered by Mr. Nott on his return. (Mr. Nott was attending a NATO meeting in Colorado Springs, from which he returned the following day.)

195. During the day there were further diplomatic exchanges with Argentina, both in London with the Argentine *Chargé d'Affaires,* Sr. Molteni, and in Buenos Aires. Foreign and Commonwealth Office officials briefed Lord Carrington and Mr. Luce on Dr. Costa Mendez's unhelpful response to the request for the Argentine Government to remove urgently the remaining personnel from South Georgia and on the report about the deployment of Argentine warships to prevent their evacuation by *HMS Endurance.* They told them that the Ministry of Defence was urgently assessing the defence implications but that, unless the problem could be resolved by diplomatic action, there was a real risk of military confrontation, which Britain was in no position to win. Lord Carrington agreed that the British Ambassador in Buenos Aires should be instructed to urge Dr. Costa Mendez strongly to persuade his colleagues to find a way out of the impasse, and to say that the British Government did not wish to escalate the situation but that the Argentine Government should be in no doubt that " we are committed to the defence of British sovereignty in South Georgia as elsewhere ". The British Ambassador in Buenos Aires was also asked to sound out Dr. Costa Mendez on whether a personal message from the Prime Minister to President Galtieri or the visit of a special representative of Lord Carrington would help.

196. These points were also made by the Foreign and Commonwealth Office to the Argentine *Chargé d'Affaires* in London, who made the personal suggestion that it might help if the British Government were to send a positive response to the proposal made at the New York talks for a permanent negotiating commission. Foreign and Commonwealth Office officials advised Ministers that sending Lord Carrington's proposed message to Dr. Costa Mendez (see paragraph 187) at that stage might only exacerbate the difficulties and that it would be better to leave the Argentines with the impression that a reply on negotiations depended on clearing up the impasse on South Georgia.

197. In the afternoon the Foreign and Commonwealth Office briefed the British Ambassador in Washington on the situation by telegram. It explained that there was a grave danger of any conflict spreading more widely and that action against the Falklands could not be discounted. The telegram also said that, while everything was being done to defuse the potentially dangerous situation, " in the final analysis we cannot acquiesce in this infringement of British sovereignty and are bound to take action to restore the *status quo* ". At the same time Foreign and Commonwealth Office officials briefed the United States *Chargé d'Affaires* in London, Mr. Streator, who undertook to report the British concern to Washington immediately.

198. The British Ambassador in Buenos Aires reported that afternoon that he had carried out his instructions at meetings with both Sr. Ros and Dr. Costa Mendez. They had both referred to articles in the British press about *HMS Endurance's* having been sent to South Georgia to take off the Argentine party there and had said that there now seemed to be no way in which the Argentines could remove the men, even if they had agreed to do so, without appearing to have responded to threats. Dr. Costa Mendez had also rejected the offers of a message from the Prime Minister and of a special representative. He had, however, asked whether the expulsion order could be revoked if Sr. Davidoff ordered his men to complete the necessary landing formalities by having their ' white cards '([1]) stamped at Grytviken. The British Ambassador recommended this course of action in view of the risk of military confrontation. Commenting on the British Ambassador's report, the Governor pointed out that the Dependencies were not included in the 1971 Communications Agreement (and were therefore outside the ' white card ' régime) and that, if the Ministry of Foreign Affairs had issued ' white cards ', this indicated its involvement in Sr. Davidoff's plans. But he agreed (in a telegram the following day) that this was the most sensible course of action, although it would be unpopular with the Islanders, provided that it was on the basis of stamping the Argentines' passports rather than their ' white cards '. A reply approved by Ministers was sent to the British Ambassador informing him that the British Government were publicly committed to the Argentines' leaving Leith. He was instructed to tell Dr. Costa Mendez that as an ultimate effort of goodwill, if the Argentine party went to Grytviken, documentation would be issued to enable it to return to Leith. The British Ambassador saw Dr. Costa Mendez in the evening. Dr. Costa Mendez told him that he could not comment on the proposal without consulting the President, which he would do and report back to the Ambassador, if possible the same evening.

199. The Ministry of Defence reported on the situation to the Chief of Defence Staff, who was abroad. It informed him that the Argentine Ministry of Foreign Affairs appeared to be trying to cool the situation, but that the Argentine Navy were taking a hard line. Two Argentine frigates, with Exocet missiles, had been deployed between South Georgia and the Falklands. The Foreign and Commonwealth Office was informed by the Prime Minister's office of her agreement to Lord Carrington's proposal that officials should urgently take forward civil contingency planning for a sea service.

([1]) The ' white card ' was a document issued by the Argentine Government for travel between Argentina and the Falkland Islands agreed as part of the 1971 Communications Agreement (see paragraph 26).

200. Reports were received during the day indicating that the Argentine forces were being kept informed about the Royal Marines on the Falkland Islands, about the movements of *HMS Endurance* and other Royal Navy ships, and also about the latest diplomatic situation. The reports indicated that it had been decided that the civilians should remain on South Georgia.

Friday 26 March

201. On 26 March the Governor informed the Foreign and Commonwealth Office that *HMS Endurance* had reported that the *Bahia Paraiso* had left Leith, but it was not yet possible to tell whether it had taken the party off. *HMS Endurance* later signalled that the Argentines were still ashore at Leith and, from the large quantity of stores visible, appeared to be established for a long stay. Captain Barker added that in his view the operation must have been planned for some time as the *Bahia Paraiso* had arrived from Antarctica, not from Argentina.

202. The British Ambassador in Buenos Aires reported that he had been told that President Galtieri wished to discuss South Georgia with the Argentine Commanders-in-Chief and that a response to the British proposal would probably not be made until the evening. In the meantime, Foreign and Commonwealth Office officials made a submission to Mr. Luce about the options, on the assumptions that the Argentines had no intention of departing and that the proposal to complete the arrangements at Grytviken was rejected. The submission said that the present evidence was that the Argentines were consolidating the landing at Leith but there was still no evidence of an Argentine military capability there. The option of preparing a task force to support *HMS Endurance* was mentioned—but not recommended at that stage—with the comment that the Ministry of Defence would not be in favour of it.

203. On Mr. Luce's advice Lord Carrington decided over the weekend that *HMS Endurance* should evacuate the Argentines but should offer to transfer them to an Argentine vessel if challenged; and that a message should be sent to Mr. Haig seeking the good offices of the United States as a mediator. Foreign and Commonwealth Office Ministers also agreed to take advantage of the arrival of a new party of Royal Marines to double-bank the garrison at Port Stanley pending the outcome of events in South Georgia.

204. Ministry of Defence officials briefed Mr. Wiggin, the Parliamentary Under-Secretary of State, Armed Forces, about the possible retention of *HMS Endurance* and about the situation in South Georgia. After consulting Mr. Nott by telephone, Mr. Wiggin wrote to Lord Carrington agreeing to the retention on station of *HMS Endurance* for the time being and informing him that arrangements were also being made to sail a support vessel on 29 March to resupply her. Mr. Wiggin said that there was an urgent need to decide *HMS Endurance's* long-term future. While he accepted that she had great symbolic importance as a demonstration of commitment to the Falklands, if the Argentines were to bring to bear the sizeable naval forces they had available, *HMS Endurance* could make only a very limited contribution to the defence of the Falklands. The Ministry of Defence could not justify paying for her retention. Mr. Wiggin added

58

that for these reasons there was everything to be said for a very early discussion by the Defence Committee, hopefully before Easter. Mr. Wiggin separately notified Mr. Luce of his agreement to the double-banking of the Port Stanley garrison.

205. The Ministry of Defence also sent to the Prime Minister's office a revised version of the note approved by the Chiefs of Staff in September 1981 on the defence implications of Argentine action against the Falkland Islands (see paragraphs 110–112). The only significant changes from the earlier version were the removal of the cost estimates and of a concluding summary paragraph, and the addition of a passage discussing the possibility, at the outset of a period of rising tension with the prospect of Argentine military action against the Falklands, of deploying a nuclear-powered submarine to the region, either covertly or overtly as a deterrent pending the arrival of further naval reinforcements. On the response to an Argentine invasion of the Falkland Islands, the conclusion was unchanged: if faced with Argentine occupation of the Islands on arrival, there could be no certainty that the large balanced force required to deter a full-scale invasion could retake them.

206. Intelligence reports were circulated—and seen by Mr. Luce—indicating that on 23 March there was still no serious intention of invasion by the Argentine Government as a whole, although there was a more hawkish attitude in Navy quarters, and that the Ministry of Foreign Affairs believed that a negotiated solution would be preferable. The reports also indicated that the Argentine Government would try to raise the temperature but would stop short of bloodshed. The British Embassy in Buenos Aires reported, on the basis of information from another Embassy, that all the submarines at the naval base of Mar del Plata had recently put to sea but that this might not be sinister since a joint naval exercise was taking place, probably in the River Plate area, with the Uruguayan navy.

Saturday 27 March

207. On Saturday 27 March the British Ambassador in Buenos Aires reported his fears that Dr. Costa Mendez had been less than honest with him and that the Argentines had been " playing us along ". He took this view because after the Commanders-in-Chief's meeting the previous evening Dr. Costa Mendez did not summon him, as they had agreed, but instead made a public statement that a firm decision had been taken to give the men on South Georgia all necessary protection, which, in view of the presence of the *Bahia Paraiso*, would not be only diplomatic. The British Ambassador reported that he was seeking an urgent interview with Dr. Costa Mendez to discuss this statement and to clarify the status of the *Bahia Paraiso*. He later saw Sr. Ros and pressed for information about the position of the *Bahia Paraiso* and about suggestions in the press that there were armed marines on board. Sr. Ros was unable to answer these questions and said that, following the Commanders-in-Chief's meeting the previous evening, revised instructions had been given to the Ministry of Foreign Affairs, which would be put into a message to the British Government and delivered that day. The British Ambassador in Buenos Aires commented later in the day that he suspected that Argentine intentions were still a subject for debate within the Junta, the navy being the most, and the army and the President

59

the least, hawkish. He said that there was still a possibility that action to remove the party from Leith would be taken as a trigger for armed action by the Argentines.

208. The British Naval *Attaché* in Buenos Aires reported Argentine press reports the previous day of a joint Argentine/Uruguayan anti-submarine exercise and the sailing of a destroyer and corvette from Mar del Plata. He had been aware of the exercise and thought that it was probably genuine. He also reported press articles that day about intense naval activity at Puerto Belgrano, the sailing of various ships, including a submarine, and the embarkation of marines. *HMS Endurance* confirmed that the *Bahia Paraiso* had sailed from Leith, but reported Argentine activity there and the continued presence of a French yacht, whose crew appeared to be working with the Argentines.

Sunday 28 March

209. On Sunday 28 March the British Ambassador in Buenos Aires reported the text of Dr. Costa Mendez's reply, which was as follows:

" The events which have taken place on St. Peter's Island in the South Georgias are being followed by my Government with close attention. I am convinced that both the British Government and Your Excellency share our concern and this is why I am sending this message with the object of dispelling any misunderstanding about my Government's motives.

" The activities of the group of workers disembarked at Leith are of a private and peaceful character based on the undisputed fact that they were known in advance by Her Britannic Majesty's Government and in any case on the fact that they are being carried out on territory subject to the special regime agreed in 1971 between the Argentine and Great Britain. It is moreover within Your Excellency's knowledge that these territories are considered by the Argentine Republic as her own and that the sovereignty dispute about them had been recognised by the United Nations in its relevant Resolutions. Your Excellency's Government has accepted the existence of the sovereignty dispute.

" However the British Government has reacted in terms which constitute a virtual ultimatum backed by the threat of military action in the form of the despatch of the naval warship *Endurance* and a requirement for the peremptorily immediate evacuation of the Argentine workers from the Island. These actions have been taken without regard to the special characteristics mentioned above. The reaction to which I refer thus constitutes a disproportionate and provocative response aggravated for having received wide diffusion in the press which has had a negative effect on developments and which is not the responsibility of the Argentine Government. In this connection I cannot but refer to the comments published in the British press many of which have had an aggravating effect and in any case do not contribute to the maintenance of the desirable climate for the conduct of negotiations.

" In the light of this attitude my Government can only adopt those measures which prudence and its rights demand. In this context the Argentine workers in South Georgia must remain there since they have been given the necessary documentation to do so.

" I feel I must point out to Your Excellency that the present situation is the direct result of the persistent lack of recognition by the United Kingdom of the titles to sovereignty which my country has over the Malvinas, South Georgia and the South Sandwich Islands. This is confirmed by the negative attitude of Your Excellency's Government throughout many years of negotiations in which Argentina has given adequate evidence of its wish to resolve the dispute by peaceful means with imagination and patience which today have lasted for over fifteen years.

" To resolve the present situation I consider it necessary that Your Excellency's Government should display, as does the Argentine Government, the political will to negotiate not only the current problem which concerns us but also the sovereignty dispute bearing in mind that so long as this continues our relations will be open to similar disturbances and crises.

" Your Excellency can be sure of counting upon the co-operation and goodwill of my Government to achieve a satisfactory solution."

The British Ambassador commented that the message did not suggest any constructive way of proceeding and withdrew Dr. Costa Mendez's proposal for the completion of formalities at Grytviken. He concluded that the Argentines intended no move to resolve the dispute, but to let matters ride while they built up their naval strength in the area. The Governor pointed out that the message contained some inaccuracies, which indicated that the Argentines either misunderstood or were flouting the 1971 Communications Agreement. He thought that the message confirmed the Argentine Government's complicity with Sr. Davidoff.

210. *HMS Endurance* reported that the *Bahia Paraiso* was stationed 15 miles off the north coast of South Georgia and that there appeared to be more than a dozen, possibly 18, Argentines at Leith.

211. In the evening, Lord Carrington sent Mr. Haig the message referred to in paragraph 203. It said that it was the British Government's firm wish to resolve the problem peacefully, but that the continued presence of the Argentines was an infringement of British sovereignty " in which we could not acquiesce ". It asked Mr. Haig to consider taking the matter up with the Argentines and suggested that the matter could be resolved either by the Argentines' seeking permission at Grytviken to regularise their position or by their evacuation by a third country ship.

212. Later that evening the Prime Minister, prompted by the most recent telegrams, telephoned Lord Carrington expressing her concern that the Government should respond effectively to the critical situation on South Georgia and worsening relations with the Argentine Government. Lord Carrington said that a message had been sent to Mr. Haig, and that Mr. Luce was to hold a meeting with officials the next morning and would report to them at midday in Brussels, where they were due to attend a European Community meeting.

Monday 29 March

213. On the morning of Monday 29 March the Prime Minister and Lord Carrington discussed the matter on their way to Brussels. They decided that a nuclear-powered submarine should be sent to support *HMS Endurance*,

61

and this was notified to the Ministry of Defence. In reply Mr. Nott sent a telegram to the Prime Minister in Brussels confirming that contingency plans had been set in hand over the week-end in the context of developments on South Georgia, as a result of which a number of steps had been taken. As *HMS Endurance* might be required to remain at South Georgia for the foreseeable future and would begin to run short of food and other supplies in three weeks, the *RFA Fort Austin* had that day sailed from Gibraltar to replenish *HMS Endurance*. She would also be capable of providing support to other ships should they have to be sent to the area. In addition, a nuclear-powered submarine would be sent covertly to reach the Falklands by 13 April, and a second submarine would be prepared. Mr. Nott advised that it would be possible to deploy a fleet of seven destroyers and frigates then on exercise off Gibraltar which could reach the Falklands in two to three weeks, but that this would not in itself constitute a viable full-strength task force. Such a force would take about a week to assemble, which would immediately become public knowledge, and a further three weeks to reach the Falklands. As stated in his subsequent despatch,([1]) on 29 March the Commander-in-Chief Fleet ordered the Flag Officer First Flotilla, Rear Admiral Sir John Woodward, to prepare to detach a suitable group of ships from Gibraltar and to be ready to proceed to the South Atlantic if required.

214. At midday on 29 March Mr. Luce reported to Lord Carrington by telegram on his meeting that morning. He recorded the general Foreign and Commonwealth Office view that it would be premature to propose a resumption of the broader Falklands negotiations, or to send a special emissary to Buenos Aires, before a further diplomatic effort had been made to resolve the problem of South Georgia. Mr. Luce advised that any resumption of wider talks in New York or Buenos Aires would look too much as if the Government were negotiating under duress, even if the solution of the South Georgia problem were made the first item on any agenda. Later in the day Lord Carrington was also sent drafts of a reply to Dr. Costa Mendez, a statement to Parliament and a further message to Mr. Haig.

215. The British Ambassador in Buenos Aires reported on Argentine press treatment of the South Georgia affair, which included reports that five Argentine warships had been despatched towards South Georgia and that all naval leave had been cancelled. He expressed his concern that the Argentine Government would not only gain in popularity by taking a jingoistic stance but would be accepted as doing the right thing in taking even the most extreme measures. Although the relationship between the United States and Argentine Governments had become important, it was questionable whether it would carry the weight of suggesting an Argentine climb-down.

216. That evening the British Ambassador in Washington reported that he had called on Mr. Stoessel, the Deputy Secretary of State at the State Department, who relayed Mr. Haig's concern that there should be restraint on both sides and insistence that the United States would not take sides. The British Ambassador had replied that the Americans could surely not be neutral in a case of illegal occupation of sovereign British territory

---

([1]) The *London Gazette* (Supplement), 13 December 1982.

and left Mr. Stoessel in no doubt that, while the British Government remained anxious to keep the temperature down, they could not allow Argentina to assert a claim in this way to a British possession. Mr. Stoessel had said that, while the Americans did not have a role to play in resolving the underlying dispute over the Falkland Islands, they were nonetheless willing to use their good offices to bring about a solution to the immediate problem on South Georgia.

217. In the afternoon the Argentine *Chargé d'Affaires*, Sr. Molteni, called on Mr. Fearn to obtain reactions to Dr. Costa Mendez's message. He said that in his view the solution of regularising the position of the Argentines at Grytviken had been foreclosed since the despatch of *HMS Endurance* to the area and the consequent escalation of the issue. He referred to pressure from " die-hards " in Argentina to capitalise on the South Georgia situation in order to resolve the whole Falklands issue by force. He thought the only probable way out of the impasse would be a positive response from the British Government to the procedural proposals for future negotiations put forward at New York. Sr. Molteni was told that this suggestion would be difficult for the British Government to accept.

218. Intelligence was received which reflected the view of Argentine officials that some form of military action stopping short of a full-scale invasion would take place in the near future and that military action was planned in April, but in the form of occupation of one of the outlying islands, not an invasion of the main islands. It indicated that the Argentine Ministry of Foreign Affairs was making an assessment of the likely reactions of members of the United Nations Security Council to Argentine occupation of the Falkland Islands. It was also learned that a beach on the Falkland Islands was to be reconnoitred by the Argentines and that an amphibious task force was being prepared.

Tuesday 30 March

219. On the morning of 30 March Lord Carrington held a meeting with Mr. Luce and officials at the Foreign and Commonwealth Office, at which the terms of a Parliamentary statement and of a reply to Dr. Costa Mendez's message of 28 March (see paragraph 209) were agreed. It was decided that the reply should propose the visit of a Foreign and Commonwealth Office official as an emissary on behalf of Lord Carrington and the resumption of negotiations on the Falklands once the South Georgia incident had been defused. The message was sent that evening (see paragraph 226).

220. In the afternoon Lord Carrington made a statement in the House of Lords[1] summarising developments in the dispute and announcing that *HMS Endurance* would remain on station for as long as was necessary.

221. Mr. Luce repeated the statement in the House of Commons.[2] In reply to questions Mr. Luce said that the Islands would be defended if necessary and that the Islanders' wishes were paramount.

222. Lord Carrington summoned Mr. Streator, the United States *Chargé d'Affaires*, to express his displeasure at the message from Mr. Haig

---

[1] *Official Report*, House of Lords, 30 March 1982, Cols. 1276–1281.
[2] *Official Report*, House of Commons, 30 March 1982, Cols. 163–170.

conveyed through Mr. Stoessel the previous day, which had put the British position on the same footing as Argentina's (see paragraph 216).

223. The British Naval *Attaché* in Buenos Aires reported to the Ministry of Defence that five Argentine warships including a submarine were sailing to South Georgia; that another four warships had sailed from Puerto Belgrano; and that travel restrictions had been imposed on personnel there. One Argentine newspaper had reported that the four warships were part of a routine training exercise, but another had stated that there had been a rush to put missiles aboard one of them.

224. Later in the afternoon of 30 March the Ministry of Defence convened a meeting of the Defence Operations Executive, which acts, when the need arises, as the executive agency on behalf of the Chiefs of Staff for the central direction of military operations. The Executive noted the position of Argentine naval ships near South Georgia and of a naval task force, comprising an aircraft carrier, four destroyers and an amphibious landing ship on exercise 800–900 miles north of the Falklands, which was unusual for that time of year. It also noted that there had been no noticeable change in Argentine Air Force readiness and that the Argentine air service to Port Stanley was continuing normally. The Foreign and Commonwealth Office advice at the meeting was that there was an indication that the Argentines planned to occupy at least one island in the Falklands some time in April. They favoured sending one or more nuclear-powered submarines. As a result of the meeting a submission was made to Mr. Nott recommending against the deployment of surface ships, which was likely to prove provocative and would require a carrier to provide air support, and against sending a third nuclear-powered submarine. It pointed out that to maintain a presence in the Falklands area for a prolonged period would make enormous demands on military resources, which would have a very serious effect on the ability to meet other commitments worldwide and would incur substantial operating costs. It also noted that the approach of winter in the area would limit the ability effectively to reinforce the Falklands.

225. Lord Carrington and Mr. Blaker, the Minister of State, Armed Forces, sent a joint minute to the Prime Minister outlining the precautionary steps which had been taken to reinforce the British naval presence in the Falklands area and what else might be done. They reported that, in addition to doubling the Royal Marine garrison at Port Stanley, sending the *RFA Fort Austin* to resupply *HMS Endurance* and sailing a nuclear-powered submarine, it had been decided that morning to confirm the order to send a second submarine. Consideration had been given to sending a third submarine. This action was favoured by Lord Carrington, and a submarine had been earmarked. But it had not yet been given orders to sail since the Ministry of Defence took the view that there would be significant operational penalties elsewhere. The minute also recorded that the possibility of sending the group of seven warships exercising off Gibraltar had been considered but was not thought advisable. The despatch of the force would become known, which would complicate the diplomatic efforts to defuse the situation, and there were military reservations about the adequacy of such a force, which could be easily matched by the Argentines. A credible force would need to be much larger; it would take about 24 days to muster and arrive in the area and would

be difficult and expensive to maintain. Its preparation, which could not be concealed, would be highly provocative and escalatory unless the Argentines were preparing to invade the Falklands, of which there was no sign. It was suggested that these matters should be discussed at the meeting of the Defence Committee arranged for Thursday 1 April.

226. In the evening of 30 March the British Ambassador was instructed to deliver a message from Lord Carrington to Dr. Costa Mendez about South Georgia. The message said that the potentially dangerous situation which had now developed had not been of the British Government's seeking. The British objective throughout had been to seek a solution acceptable to both Governments. A confrontation, which could have far reaching consequences and which could seriously prejudice attempts to resolve the whole Falklands issue through peaceful negotiation, was in the interests of neither Government. The message proposed sending a senior Foreign and Commonwealth Office official (Mr. Ure) as a personal emissary on his behalf to Buenos Aires with constructive proposals for a solution allowing the salvage contract on South Georgia to be carried out. It said that Lord Carrington would view the defusing of the South Georgia incident as preparing the way for a resumption of the dialogue on the broader issues discussed between Mr. Luce and Sr. Ros in New York in February.

227. The same evening the British Ambassador in Buenos Aires reported the United States' Ambassador's account of Dr. Costa Mendez's wholly negative reaction to the approach he had made on the instructions of Mr. Stoessel, the Deputy Secretary of State at the State Department. Dr. Costa Mendez had said that the United States' good offices, while welcome on the underlying dispute, were not required on the current incident and that the compromises suggested by them were not acceptable. There would be no confrontation, provided the British did nothing to disturb the Argentine workmen. The solution of the problem of the incident could be found in starting without delay on negotiation of the main dispute. The British Ambassador noted that this uncompromising stand was taken a few hours before major demonstrations in Buenos Aires by labour unions against the Government's austerity measures. It was generally believed there that the Government had been hoping that the recent jingoist fervour would decide the unions to put off the demonstrations or at least steal the headlines. It also seemed to show Dr. Costa Mendez repeating a formula given him in advance to use without discretion. It seemed that the Argentine Government had their tails up and believed that they had found a way of bullying Britain into conceding sovereignty. However, that mood might not last for long. Commenting on his instructions from Lord Carrington, the British Ambassador advised against sending a special emissary and against passing on the message to Dr. Costa Mendez at that stage, on the grounds that it had so far been possible for him to maintain civil relations with the Argentines without conceding ground, and a conciliatory gesture and message at that time might serve to convince the Argentines that they had the British Government on the run, not only over South Georgia but over conceding sovereignty. He suggested holding up the message for a day or two while considering the United States' reaction to the report of their Ambassador in Buenos Aires.

228. Later that evening, the Foreign and Commonwealth Office sent a telegram to Lord Carrington, who was then in Israel, about two

65

intelligence reports received since his departure reflecting Argentine service views. One indicated that a peaceful settlement of the South Georgia incident was possible but that, if any Argentines were killed, Argentina would initiate military action against the Falkland Islands themselves. The Argentine Government had not provoked the South Georgia incident but, now that it had happened, would take advantage of it to press forward Argentina's claim to sovereignty over all the islands. The Argentine assessment was that, while Britain might send naval reinforcements to the area, this was unlikely. The other report indicated that the Argentine Government could take military action against the Falklands in April, not through a complete invasion, but by occupying one of the outlying islands. A further report indicated that the Argentine Navy was keeping under review British naval dispositions worldwide.

Wednesday 31 March

229. On the morning of Wednesday 31 March Lord Carrington sent a telegram from Tel Aviv accepting the advice of the British Ambassador in Buenos Aires to delay the message to Dr. Costa Mendez. Later in the day, however, Lord Carrington decided that the message should be delivered, in view both of the intelligence reports and of a British press report that day about the sailing of a nuclear-powered submarine, which might give the Argentines the impression that the British were seeking a naval rather than a diplomatic solution. The British Ambassador in Buenos Aires was instructed accordingly, and he delivered the message that evening.

230. An immediate assessment headed " Falkland Islands—the incident on South Georgia " was prepared and circulated by the Latin America Current Intelligence Group. It assessed that the landing on South Georgia had not been contrived by the Argentine Government, but that the Junta was taking full advantage of the incident to speed up negotiations on the transfer of sovereignty. Despite Sr. Davidoff's close contacts with some senior Argentine naval officers, the unauthorised landing was not considered to be part of the Navy's plans. There was no central co-ordination of Argentine policy and the Junta's intentions were not known, but it had a wide range of options open to it. Argentina had overwhelming superiority in the area. There was a possibility that, both because of the strength of Argentine public feeling on the issue and because of imperfect co-ordination and the confused counsel given by various Argentine officials and service advisers, the Junta might take some unexpected action. The assessment concluded that the Argentine Junta's main aim in its handling of the Falkland Islands dispute was to persuade the British Government to negotiate the transfer of sovereignty, and it was likely to try to use the incident on South Georgia to obtain the early opening of talks on the basis discussed in New York in February. This would tend to constrain it from adopting extreme options, but the possibility could not be ruled out that it might in future choose to escalate the situation by landing a military force on another Dependency or on one of the Falkland Islands. But it was believed that at that time the Argentine Government did not wish to be the first to adopt forcible measures. There was, however, a high risk of the Argentine Government's resorting to the use of force to rescue their nationals if the Argentine civilians on South Georgia were arrested or removed from the island. The Argentine Government would

see such action by the British authorities as highly provocative and might use it as a pretext for an invasion of the Falkland Islands.

231. The British Naval *Attaché* in Buenos Aires reported to the Ministry of Defence that, according to the United States Naval *Attaché,* virtually all the Argentine fleet was at sea, but without the fleet commanders, and that this was well in advance of the next exercises planned for after Easter.

232. The British Ambassador in Buenos Aires reported Argentine press comment on the dispute, which had been overshadowed by violent demonstrations in Buenos Aires against the Government's economic policies. Lord Carrington's statement had been reported, but the popular press had given greater prominence to the despatch of a nuclear-powered submarine. There were also reports of the despatch of a British destroyer and a Royal Fleet Auxiliary vessel. Dr. Costa Mendez was widely quoted as telling reporters that Argentina would not give way to threats of force and that the group on South Georgia was on Argentine soil.

233. In the early evening of 31 March Mr. Nott was briefed by Ministry of Defence officials on intelligence which had been received that day that a time in the early morning of 2 April had been set by the Argentines as the time and day for action. It was considered that, taken with earlier intelligence reports, this provided a positive indication of an Argentine intention to invade the Falkland Islands. These reports were also seen by the Foreign and Commonwealth Office and the Joint Intelligence Organisation.

234. Mr. Nott sought, and obtained, an urgent meeting with the Prime Minister, which took place in her room at the House of Commons. It was also attended by Mr. Atkins, Mr. Luce, and Foreign and Commonwealth Office and Ministry of Defence officials. The Chief of Naval Staff was also present, having gone to the House of Commons to brief Mr. Nott.

235. At the meeting a message from the Prime Minister to President Reagan was drafted and sent just before 9.00 p.m. In it the Prime Minister referred to intelligence indicating that an Argentine invasion of the Falklands might be imminent and said that the British Government could not acquiesce in any Argentine occupation. She asked President Reagan to talk urgently to President Galtieri and ask for an immediate assurance that he would not authorise any landing, let alone hostilities; she said that he could tell President Galtieri that the British Government would not escalate the dispute or start fighting. The British Ambassador in Washington was asked to speak to Mr. Haig to ensure a rapid reaction from the White House. The Chief of Naval Staff advised on the size and composition of a task force likely to be capable of re-taking the Islands and was instructed to prepare such a force without commitment to a final decision as to whether or not it should sail.

236. The Foreign and Commonwealth Office immediately informed the British Ambassador in Buenos Aires and the Governor of the Falklands of the reports indicating a possible invasion. The Governor was instructed to pass on this information only to the garrison commander, *HMS Endurance* was ordered back to Port Stanley.

237. At 10.30 p.m. the British Ambassador in Buenos Aires delivered the message (see paragraph 229) to Dr. Costa Mendez, who said that he would communicate the message to his President and report back. Dr. Costa Mendez added, however, that the message was not what he had hoped for.

He agreed on the need to avoid confrontation, but said that the statements in Parliament and the press reports of warship movements did not encourage hope for a quick solution.

238. Intelligence indicated that the Argentine Ministry of Foreign Affairs thought that the minimum acceptable reply from the British Government would be an agreement to enter into immediate negotiations on sovereignty and that Argentina would not now give up its presence on South Georgia. It also indicated that Dr. Costa Mendez was being used by the Junta as nothing more than an adviser over South Georgia; and that the Argentine Navy had asked for a forecast of voting in the United Nations Security Council in the event of a military initiative against the Falklands. Dr. Costa Mendez was said to have advised the Junta on 26 March that there would be a balance of votes against Argentina. There was also a report of preparations for the disembarkation of a marine infantry brigade.

Thursday 1 April

239. The British Ambassador in Washington reported having seen Mr. Haig. He had outlined to him the intelligence reports of Argentine intentions, the significance of which Mr. Haig had been unaware.

240. At 9.30 a.m. the Cabinet met. In Lord Carrington's absence, Mr. Atkins reported the latest developments on South Georgia, the diplomatic efforts being made, and the deployment of Argentine naval forces. He advised that, while certain precautionary measures had been taken, it would not be an easy task to defend the Falklands. Summing up the discussion, the Prime Minister said that the best hope of avoiding confrontation lay in the influence that the United States Government could bring to bear on the Argentine Government.

241. At the same time an assessment prepared by the Latin America Current Intelligence Group was circulated updating the information about Argentine military dispositions, which would enable Argentina to launch an assault on 2 April. The destination, although not known for certain, appeared to be Port Stanley. The assessment said that, despite these military preparations, there was no intelligence suggesting that the Argentine Junta had taken a decision to invade the Falkland Islands. The evidence of unusual co-operation between the three Argentine military services and their active involvement in the amphibious task force was disturbing. The report judged that the assembled Argentine force now had the capability and logistic support necessary for an invasion of part of the Falkland Islands and that it would be in a position from which it could launch an assault by about the middle of the day on Friday 2 April.

242. Later in the morning of 1 April the Defence Committee met to consider the precautionary military deployments in hand for the Falkland Islands. The Prime Minister informed the Committee that an Argentine task force could reach Port Stanley during the morning of 2 April, but that the Argentine Government's precise intentions were not known. A diplomatic solution had to be found if possible, and the United States Government would be making representations at the highest level. As it was far from clear that Argentina would be willing to agree to a diplomatic solution, preparations had to be made against the possibilities that it would

cut off services to the Islands or that some kind of military invasion might occur. In discussion, the British naval deployments already made were noted, and attention was drawn to the fact that a very large naval task force of surface ships would be required to deal with the Argentine force. The size of the Argentine force, the distances involved, and the importance of avoiding any action which would endanger the Islanders meant that there was no alternative for the moment to seeking to resolve the problem by diplomatic means. The Committee agreed that every effort should continue to be made to resolve the current dispute with Argentina by diplomatic means. The United States Government had been assured that the British Government would not take any early action amounting to an escalation of the situation. The Committee also agreed that *HMS Endurance* should not be withdrawn as earlier planned, but for the time being should remain on station in the South Atlantic. Officials were authorised urgently to make contingency plans for alternative services to those provided by Argentina, including the replacement of the weekly air service between Argentina and the Falkland Islands, probably by a sea service direct to the United Kingdom. The Committee also agreed not to send troops to reinforce the garrison at Port Stanley since they would not arrive in time or in sufficient strength to resist an invasion and their despatch might trigger an immediate Argentine landing.

243. Mr. Streator, the United States *Chargé d'Affaires,* delivered a message from Mr. Haig to Lord Carrington undertaking that the United States Government would do all it could to help. Mr. Haig said that the United States Ambassador in Buenos Aires had been instructed to urge Dr. Costa Mendez to take no steps which would aggravate the crisis. Mr. Haig added that he thought that the United States would have a greater chance of influencing Argentine behaviour if they appeared not to favour one side or the other. Later in the day Mr. Streator delivered a message to the Prime Minister from President Reagan saying that his Government shared British concern about apparent moves against the Falkland Islands and would contact the Argentine Government at the highest levels to urge them not to take military action.

244. In the afternoon of 1 April, the British Ambassador in Buenos Aires reported his interview with Dr. Costa Mendez, who had told him that the Argentine Government regarded the South Georgia incident as closed. The British Ambassador asked for a written statement of the Argentine position, which was given to him in the following terms:

" Since the problem raised is disregard of Argentine sovereignty,

— I judge pointless the despatch of a person to examine the events in the Georgias since Argentina considers this incident resolved. In fact the workers there are carrying out their tasks under normal lawful conditions without any breach of the agreement previously reached between our two countries

— bearing in mind the antecedents and course of the negotiations undertaken from 1964 to today we would have accepted the despatch of the representative proposed by Great Britain if his task had been to negotiate the modalities of transferring sovereignty over the Malvinas Islands and their dependencies to the Argentine Republic which is essentially the central cause of the present difficulties.

I cannot omit to draw attention to the unusual British naval deployment towards our waters reported in the international press which can only be interpreted as an unacceptable threat of the use of military force. This obliges us to refer to the UN organisation where Argentina will circulate a note on the antecedents of this case."

245. The British Defence *Attaché* in Buenos Aires reported Argentine press statements that Air Force transport aircraft were being prepared to lift troops to the south of the country. The British Ambassador later reported details of further Argentine press statements about the mobilisation of ships and troops and about intentions to widen the scope of the South Georgia incident.

246. In the early evening of 1 April the British Ambassador to the United Nations, who had been in close touch with the Foreign and Commonwealth Office, reported the success of an initiative, which had led to the Secretary-General's summoning both the Argentine and British Ambassadors to express his concern about rising tension. The Secretary-General would be making a public appeal to both sides to settle their differences through diplomatic means. The British Ambassador prepared a draft statement to the Security Council calling on it to take immediate action to prevent an invasion, and a draft Resolution calling on the Argentine Government to exercise the utmost restraint and to refrain from the use or threat of force in the South Atlantic. It was later agreed with the President of the Council that, instead of the Resolution, he would make a Presidential statement. The British Ambassador subsequently reported that he thought as much action as possible by the Security Council had been achieved. There had been two appeals by the Secretary-General and a firm Presidential statement, and Britain had the sympathy of the majority of the Council. The Argentine Ambassador to the United Nations had, however, ignored his appeal to join Britain in a positive response to the Council's call for restraint.

247. The Foreign and Commonwealth Office informed the Governor of the Falkland Islands and the British Ambassadors in Washington, New York and Buenos Aires, that there was reliable information that an Argentine naval task force would be assembling off Port Stanley the next morning.

248. The British Ambassador in Washington informed the Foreign and Commonwealth Office that the United States Ambassador in Buenos Aires had spoken to Dr. Costa Mendez that morning; that Dr. Costa Mendez had been non-committal; and that the United States Ambassador had arranged to see President Galtieri in the afternoon to deliver a message from Mr. Haig with President Reagan's authority. The British Ambassador later reported that, at the meeting with the United States Ambassador, President Galtieri would not say what Argentina was going to do, but had talked about the need for the British to discuss surrendering sovereignty. The United States Ambassador had concluded that Argentina would go through with its military operation. The State Department would now ask President Reagan to talk personally to President Galtieri.

249. The Governor reported on the arrangements made for the deployment of the Royal Marines, and consulted the Foreign and Commonwealth Office about informing the civilian population and rounding

up local Argentines. The Foreign and Commonwealth Office pointed out that, while the evidence of Argentine intentions to attack the next day was highly suggestive, it was not yet entirely conclusive and diplomatic action was being taken to prevent an attack.

250. Intelligence received on 1 April indicated that at the end of March the military leaders in Argentina were close to using the military option to solve the dispute with Britain and had decided to invade the Falklands if no constructive proposal was forthcoming from the British Government by the end of the week. The constructive proposal would have to involve a concrete agreement to talk about the transfer of sovereignty within a set period. The military option could be put into action on 3 or 4 April.

251. At a meeting later in the evening of 1 April between the Prime Minister, Lord Carrington and Mr. Nott, it was decided that troops should be put on immediate notice for deployment to the South Atlantic. They noted that the naval task force assembling in British ports was at four hours' notice to sail within the next 48 hours, and that the ships exercising off Gibraltar were moving south; they would not act independently but would form up with the force assembling in British ports if it sailed.

Friday 2 April

252. In the early hours of Friday 2 April Mr. Haig informed Lord Carrington that President Galtieri had refused to receive President Reagan's telephone call. The President's message was, however, being sent to Buenos Aires immediately and would be delivered within the hour. Mr. Haig was trying to reach Dr. Costa Mendez on the telephone and the Argentine Ambassador in Washington was being summoned. The Vatican had also been contacted and was trying to get a message to President Galtieri.

253. At about the same time intelligence was received that orders had been issued on 1 April for the Argentine occupation of the Falklands and Grytviken.

254. Eventually President Reagan succeeded in speaking to President Galtieri. At 2.45 a.m. he sent the Prime Minister a message reporting on his telephone conversation, in which he said that President Galtieri had spoken in terms of ultimatums and had left him with the clear impression that he was embarked on a course of armed conflict.

255. A fuller account of President Reagan's initiative was received later on 2 April. Early the previous evening the United States President had tried to telephone the Argentine President, who initially refused to take the call. When President Reagan eventually spoke to him, he had urged in forceful terms that Argentina should not take action against the Falklands, which he said the British would regard as a *casus belli*. He had left President Galtieri in no doubt of the consequences of such action on relations between Argentina and the United States. President Galtieri emphatically rejected President Reagan's offer to send Vice-President Bush immediately to Buenos Aires to assist in a solution.

256. At 9.45 a.m. the Prime Minister informed the Cabinet that an Argentine invasion appeared imminent. Mr. Nott reported that a large

amphibious task force had been put on immediate alert. Lord Carrington reported the continuing diplomatic initiatives. It was agreed that a decision to instruct the task force to sail should be considered later.

257. At midday *RRS Bransfield*, a British Antarctic Survey ship, reported interruptions of local Falkland Islands radio broadcasts confirming that Argentines had landed. There were also reports of invasion from the State Department, from the British Antarctic Survey station at Grytviken and from the Cable and Wireless operator in Port Stanley.

258. At 7.30 p.m. the Cabinet met and agreed that the task force should sail.

259. On Saturday 3 April, the Prime Minister announced in the House of Commons([1]) that Argentina's armed forces had attacked the Falkland Islands the previous day and established military control of the Islands.

([1]) *Official Report*, House of Commons, 3 April 1982, Cols. 633–668.

CHAPTER 4

THE GOVERNMENT'S DISCHARGE OF THEIR
RESPONSIBILITIES

260. In this Chapter we address the central issue of our terms of reference, the way in which the responsibilities of Government in relation to the Falkland Islands and the Falkland Islands Dependencies were discharged in the period leading up to the invasion. We have had to consider many questions, but two are crucial. First, could the Government have foreseen the invasion on 2 April? Secondly, could the Government have prevented that invasion? We deal with the first question at the outset of the Chapter. The second question is more complex and in our view cannot be answered until we have examined how the dispute became critical and how it was handled at various stages by the present Government. We consider the answer to this question at the end of the Chapter.

Could the invasion of 2 April have been foreseen?

261. We consider first the question whether before 31 March the Government had warning of the invasion of the Falkland Islands on 2 April. We have described in detail in Chapter 3 the events of the days leading up to the invasion and all the information available at the time, including all relevant reports from the intelligence agencies. We believe that our account demonstrates conclusively that the Government had no reason to believe before 31 March that an invasion of the Falkland Islands would take place at the beginning of April.

262. All the information, including intelligence reports, that has come to light since the invasion suggests that the decision to invade was taken by the Junta at a very late date.

263. Argentine naval forces were at sea between about 23 and 28 March, in the course of annual naval exercises, which included a joint anti-submarine exercise with Uruguay (press accounts of which the British Naval *Attaché* in Buenos Aires reported on 27 March). The Argentine news agency reported on 2 April that the fleet had sailed south from Puerto Belgrano on 28 March with a marine infantry battalion, an amphibious command section and troops embarked. The actual order to invade was probably not given until at least 31 March, and possibly as late as 1 April. Dr. Costa Mendez was subsequently reported as saying that the Junta did not finally decide on the invasion until 10.00 p.m. (7.00 p.m. local time) on 1 April. It is probable that the decision to invade was taken in the light of the development of the South Georgia situation; but it seems that the violent demonstrations in Buenos Aires on the night of 30/31 March were also a factor in the Junta's decision.

264. It may be thought that, although the Government could not have had earlier warning of the invasion, they must have had fuller and more significant information of Argentine military movements. The fact is that there was no coverage of these movements and no evidence available to the Government from satellite photographs. We discuss these matters further below in the context of the arrangements made for gathering intelligence.

73

265. We specifically asked all those who gave evidence to us—Ministers and officials, the British Ambassador in Buenos Aires and other Embassy staff, the Governor of the Falkland Islands, Falkland Islanders and persons outside Government with special knowledge of and interest in the area—whether at any time up to the end of March they thought an invasion of the Falklands was likely at the beginning of April. They all stated categorically that they did not.

266. In the light of this evidence, we are satisfied that the Government did not have warning of the decision to invade. The evidence of the timing of the decision taken by the Junta shows that the Government not only did not, but could not, have had earlier warning. The invasion of the Falkland Islands on 2 April could not have been foreseen.

How did the dispute become critical?

267. Before we consider the present Government's handling of the dispute, we need to examine the question: how did the dispute develop into such a critical state that a sudden and unforeseeable invasion took place? To answer it, it is necessary to look back at the main features of the dispute and the positions of the parties to it over a longer period.

The positions of the parties to the dispute

268. From 1965 the positions of the three main parties to the dispute —the Argentine Government, the British Government and the Islanders— remained constant.

269. First, for all Argentine Governments repossession of the 'Malvinas' was always a major issue of policy and a national issue. The dispute has not held the same place in the attention of British Governments or of the British people. Although it pressed its claims with greater force on some occasions than on others, Argentina never wavered in its commitment to recover the Islands. Whatever other issues were proposed for discussion, such as economic co-operation on fisheries or oil exploration, its overriding concern was with sovereignty. In only one instance, namely the talks leading to the Communications Agreements in 1971 (see paragraphs 26–28), did Argentina take part in negotiations that were not in part concerned with some form of transfer of sovereignty. It did so in the hope that, by improving communications between the Islands and the mainland and showing its goodwill, it would persuade the Islanders of the benefits of a closer relationship between them, leading in time to constitutional changes; and it followed up the Agreements by pressing for a resumption of negotiations on sovereignty.

270. Secondly, all British Governments asserted British sovereignty over the Islands and the Dependencies, without reservation as to their title, coupled with an unchanging commitment to the defence of their territorial integrity. Although at the time of the first United Nations Resolution in 1965 the Government stated that sovereignty was not negotiable, from 1966 all British Governments were prepared to negotiate about sovereignty over the Islands, and to reach a settlement, provided that certain conditions were fulfilled and that it was capable of being carried in Parliament. The most important condition has always been that any settlement must be acceptable to the Islanders, and Ministers of successive Governments have

made unequivocal statements to Parliament to this effect. This was also always made plain to the Argentine Government.

271. Thirdly, the Islanders always made it clear that they wished to remain British and consistently resisted any change in their constitutional relationship with the United Kingdom. On occasion they acquiesced in negotiations and later took part in negotiations; but they never approved any proposals for a settlement of the sovereignty issue going beyond a lengthy freeze of the dispute. They were not prepared to agree even to the proposed scheme of joint scientific activity in the Dependencies worked out with Argentina in 1979, which they saw as a threat to British sovereignty in the area (see paragraph 69).

Developments affecting the attitude of the Argentine Government

272. While the positions of the three sides in the dispute remained constant, circumstances in Argentina changed and British Government policy developed in several important respects.

(i) Developments in Argentina.

273. In Argentina itself the military takeover in 1976 was an important factor. The *coup* placed decision-making in the hands of a small group at the head of the armed services, and increased the influence of the Navy, which had always been the most hawkish of the services on the Falklands issue. It introduced a repressive régime, whose appalling human rights record understandably increased the Islanders' reluctance to contemplate any form of closer association with Argentina. There was also a danger that the Junta might at any time seek to divert attention from domestic problems, particularly as economic difficulties grew, by appealing to Argentine nationalism to support an initiative on the Malvinas.

274. The other main issue in Argentine foreign policy over the period was its sovereignty dispute with Chile over three islands in the Beagle Channel. Argentina's concern is less with the islands themselves, which are occupied by Chile, than with their territorial waters and continental shelves, as it is strongly opposed to any extension of Chilean sovereignty into the South Atlantic. The relevance of this issue to the Falkland Islands dispute was that, if Argentina were preoccupied with the Beagle Channel dispute, it would divert its attention from the Falkland Islands; whereas, if that dispute were going in favour of Chile or reached deadlock, Argentina was more likely to seek a compensatory success in the Falklands.

275. In 1977 an International Court of Arbitration awarded the islands to Chile, but did not pronounce on the seaward extension of either side's claims. Argentina refused to accept the award, despite earlier agreement to adhere to the Court's findings, and the following year the two countries came to the brink of war on the issue. A Papal mediator was appointed, whose proposals again favoured Chile. Argentina delayed its response to his proposals, and early in 1982 announced its intention of abrogating a treaty with Chile, the effect of which would be to prevent the dispute being referred to the International Court of Justice. From Argentina's point of view the dispute had reached an impasse adverse to the Junta, and this was likely to focus its attention more closely on the Falklands.

276. A further development in Argentine foreign policy was its rapprochement with the United States from the time President Reagan's

administration took office. We referred in Chapter 2 (see paragraph 120) to evidence of improved relations between the two countries, in particular the visits that General Galtieri made to the United States in 1981, when he was Commander-in-Chief of the Army. It seems likely that the Argentine Government came to believe that the United States Government were sympathetic to their claim to the Falkland Islands and, while not supporting forcible action in furtherance of it, would not actively oppose it. When initially asked to intervene, the United States did adopt an ' even-handed ' approach, while using their good offices to attempt to find a solution.

277.   Given the relative closeness of the Falkland Islands to Argentina, their distance from Britain and the absence of a substantial British deterrent force in the area, Argentina always had the capability successfully to mount a sudden operation against the Islands. Moreover, in recent years there was a substantial increase in Argentina's military strength in all three of its armed services, which must have increased its confidence in its ability to occupy the Islands and retain them.

(ii) Developments in British policy

278.   Argentina's growing military power coincided with an increasing concentration on the part of the United Kingdom on its NATO role and the progressive restriction of its other defence commitments. Even before the Defence Review published in 1966 the South Atlantic had not been a major area of deployment, but the decisions taken in 1967 to withdraw the Commander-in-Chief, South Atlantic, and the frigate on station in the area, and in 1974 to terminate the Simonstown agreements, marked the lower priority attached to a British defence capability in the area. As the Argentine threat grew, in deciding to maintain only a token presence in the area, in the form of a small detachment of Royal Marines and in the summer months *HMS Endurance,* successive Governments had to accept that the Islands could not be defended against sudden invasion. These decisions were taken in the light of wider strategic interests, but it is likely that they were seen by Argentina as evidence of a decreasing British commitment to the defence of the Islands, however strongly that commitment was publicly asserted.

279.   Nor were these the only signals that could be read by Argentina as evidence of diminishing British interest in protecting its sovereignty in the area. Argentina no doubt always had in mind that what it saw as the weakness of Britain's response to the establishment of an Argentine presence on Southern Thule in 1976 was an indication that it might be able to mount similar operations, at least in the uninhabited islands, without provoking serious retaliatory action.

280.   There were other British Government policies which may have served to cast doubt on British commitment to the Islands and their defence. These included the Government's preparedness, subject to certain restrictions, to continue arms sales to Argentina (and to provide training facilities in the United Kingdom for Argentine military personnel); the decision not to implement some of the recommendations of Lord Shackleton's 1976 report, notably that relating to the extension of the airfield; and the failure in the British Nationality Act to extend British citizenship to those inhabitants of the Islands who either were not themselves patrial or did not have a United Kingdom-born grandparent.

281. Finally, the 1981 Defence Review may have provided further reassurance to Argentina, in view of the planned reductions in the surface fleet, the sale of *HMS Invincible* and, more particularly, the decision, although it was never implemented, to withdraw *HMS Endurance*. In short, as Argentine military power increased the British capability to respond to it became more restricted.

282. The course of negotiations over the years was also itself an important factor limiting the Government's freedom of manoeuvre. As successive initiatives had been tried and failed, and with no signs of softening of either Argentine or Islander attitudes, the picture that the history of the dispute presents is one in which the negotiating options were progressively eliminated until only one—leaseback—was left that might eventually satisfy the aspirations of Argentina on the one hand and the wishes of the Islanders on the other.

283. It is against that background that we examine the present Government's handling of the dispute. What stands out is the dilemma to which successive Governments were exposed by their policy of seeking to resolve, or at least contain, the dispute by diplomatic negotiation on the one hand and their commitment to the defence of the Falkland Islands on the other. This dilemma sharpened as the policy options diminished. The Islands were always at risk, and increasingly so as Argentina's military capability grew stronger; but a British decision to deploy to the area any additional warships, whose secrecy could not always be assured, also carried a risk, dependent on its timing, of frustrating the prospect of negotiation. This dilemma underlined the importance of the token defence presence, which we examine in the next section of this Chapter.

Did Foreign and Commonwealth Office officials pursue a policy of their own?

284. Before coming to that, however, we first deal with the allegation that over the years Foreign and Commonwealth Office officials pursued a policy aimed at getting rid of the Islands, irrespective of the views of Ministers. In our examination of the papers we have found no evidence to support this damaging allegation, and we believe it to be totally without foundation. On every occasion that a new government—or new Ministers—came into office a full range of policy options was put before them. In every case Ministers made a decision of policy and chose to seek a negotiated settlement that would be acceptable to Argentina and to the Islanders. Without exception they rejected the alternative of 'Fortress Falklands', which would have involved the isolation of the Islands from Argentina and probably from the rest of Latin America.

How did the present Government handle the dispute?

Continuity of policy and HMS Endurance

285. A chief responsibility of British Governments in relation to the Falkland Islands and the Falkland Islands Dependencies, as for any other part of British territory, is for their defence and security. As we have already explained, the policy of successive Governments on the defence of the Islands has been to maintain a token presence on the Falklands in the

form of a small detachment of Royal Marines. This force was adequate to deal with sudden 'adventurist' incursions, which up to about 1975 were regarded as the main threat.

286. Although from that time the Argentine threat of military action increased, no Government was prepared to establish a garrison on the Falklands large enough to repel a full-scale Argentine invasion, or to provide an extended runway for the airfield, with supporting facilities. A larger airfield, if it could have been afforded within Government defence priorities, might have enhanced Britain's deterrent capacity in the area; but it would not in itself have ensured rapid reinforcement by air in a crisis since, in view of the distances involved and the uncertainties of the South Atlantic weather, landing on the Falklands could not be guaranteed and, at a time of confrontation with Argentina, diversion airfields in South America were unlikely to be available (see paragraph 108). Before the invasion air reinforcement from Ascension Island, 3500 miles away, was believed to be impracticable because of the distance involved, the lack of a diversion airfield and the refuelling techniques required.

287. Throughout the period, in addition to the detachment of Royal Marines, a Royal Naval ice-patrol vessel, first *HMS Protector* and subsequently *HMS Endurance,* was kept on station in the area in the summer months. In paragraphs 114–118 we described the decision to withdraw *HMS Endurance* and the subsequent appeals by Lord Carrington to Mr. Nott to reverse it. We recognise the limited military value of this vessel; but, as the only regular Royal Naval presence in the area, her symbolic role was important in relation to Argentina. With the exception of the occasions in 1976 and 1977 (see paragraphs 45, 59 and 65–66) when the Government buttressed negotiations by undisclosed naval deployments, successive Governments relied on their negotiating policy and on diplomatic means to prevent a confrontation with Argentina; and the role of *HMS Endurance,* as a token of the Government's commitment to the defence of the Falkland Islands and Dependencies, was a valuable complement to that. That was clearly borne out by the press and intelligence reports of Argentine reactions to the decision to pay her off.

288. We conclude, in view of these factors, that it was inadvisable for the Government to announce a decision to withdraw *HMS Endurance* and that, in the light of the developing situation in the second half of 1981, they should have rescinded their decision to pay off *HMS Endurance* at the end of her 1981/82 tour.

The decisions of September 1981

289. As 1981 wore on, one of the most significant developments in the situation was the receding prospect of negotiating a leaseback solution. Mr. Ridley's meeting on 30 June 1981 was held against the background of a general belief that time was running out and that Argentine impatience was growing. It reviewed the policy options and concluded that the only feasible option was leaseback preceded by an education campaign both in the Falkland Islands and at home. At his meeting on 7 September, however, Lord Carrington decided not to pursue that course of action, but to discuss the whole matter with Dr. Camilion in New York later in the

month and to suggest to him that it would help if the Argentines were able to make constructive proposals for resolving the dispute. Lord Carrington told us that, in his view, there was no prospect of ' selling' leaseback at that stage. It did not have support in the Islands, in the House of Commons or amongst his own Ministerial colleagues in Government. So he saw this approach to Dr. Camilion as the best diplomatic tactic in the circumstances. The Government was thenceforth left with no resort other than attempting to keep negotiations going by some means or other, and they were in the position of having nothing to offer Argentina other than what the wishes of the Islanders dictated. Lord Carrington himself recognised this in his minute of 14 September 1981, in which he said that, unless and until the Islanders modified their views, there was " little we can do beyond trying to keep some sort of negotiation going ".

290. We conclude that the Government were in a position of weakness, and that the effect of Lord Carrington's decision was to pass the initiative to the Argentine Government.

291. Lord Carrington also decided on 7 September not to present a paper for collective Ministerial discussion in the Defence Committee. Instead he circulated a minute to his Defence Committee colleagues on 14 September. This was one of a series of minutes (he circulated others on 2 December 1981, 15 February 1982 and 24 March 1982) by which he kept the Prime Minister and Defence Committee colleagues informed of progress in the dispute up to the time of the invasion. We recognise that Cabinet Committees, such as the Defence Committee, usually meet to take decisions at the invitation of the Minister with proposals to put forward; and we have noted that, in September 1981, the prospect of further negotiations still existed on the basis of agreed Government policy. Nevertheless, it was also evident at the time that the policy road ahead, last endorsed by Ministers in January 1981, could well be blocked, with serious political repercussions. Officials in both the Foreign and Commonwealth Office and the Ministry of Defence were looking to Ministers to review the outcome of the contingency planning they had done in view of a potentially more aggressive posture by Argentina. In the event, Government policy towards Argentina and the Falkland Islands was never formally discussed outside the Foreign and Commonwealth Office after January 1981. Thereafter, the time was never judged to be ripe although we were told in oral evidence that, subject to the availability of Ministers, a Defence Committee meeting could have been held at any time, if necessary at short notice. There was no meeting of the Defence Committee to discuss the Falklands until 1 April 1982; and there was no reference to the Falklands in Cabinet, even after the New York talks of 26 and 27 February, until Lord Carrington reported on events in South Georgia on 25 March 1982.

292. We cannot say what the outcome of a meeting of the Defence Committee might have been, or whether the course of events would have been altered if it had met in September 1981; but, in our view, it could have been advantageous, and fully in line with Whitehall practice, for Ministers to have reviewed collectively at that time, or in the months immediately ahead, the current negotiating position; the implications of the conflict between the attitudes of the Islanders and the aims of the Junta; and the longer-term policy options in relation to the dispute.

The view in the Foreign and Commonwealth Office at the beginning of the year

293. At the beginning of 1982 there was evidence from several sources that Argentina, and particularly the new government of President Galtieri, was committed to achieving success in its Malvinas policy in a much shorter timescale than most previous Argentine Governments had envisaged. There were clear indications that it attached particular significance to achieving a solution of the dispute on its terms, in which the sovereignty issue was the overriding consideration, by January 1983, the 150th anniversary of British occupation. These indications included General Galtieri's remarks in his speech in May 1981, intelligence about the attitude of different elements in the Argentine Government, the press comment at the beginning of the year and, definitively, the terms of the *bout de papier* at the end of January 1982, which called for serious negotiations with a timescale of one year, culminating in the recognition of Argentine sovereignty.

294. The Foreign and Commonwealth Office recognised clearly that the situation was moving towards confrontation, as is shown by the advice they gave their Ministers at the beginning of the year, notably in connection with the Annual Report of the Governor of the Falkland Islands. They believed, however—and their belief was supported by evidence—first, that Argentina would not move to confrontation until negotiations broke down; secondly, that there would be a progression of measures starting with the withdrawal of Argentine services to the Islands and increased diplomatic pressure, including further action at the United Nations; and thirdly—and the intelligence bore this out—that no action, let alone invasion of the Islands, would take place before the second half of the year.

Contingency planning

295. Nevertheless, in recognition of the deteriorating situation, the Foreign and Commonwealth Office had set in hand in 1981 contingency plans to provide alternative services for the Islands, and, at its request, the Ministry of Defence prepared a paper on the military options available in response to possible aggressive action by Argentina (see paragraph 110). A paper on civil contingency planning was also prepared in September 1981 in expectation of a meeting of the Defence Committee, at which Ministerial authority might have been obtained to take the plans further. Chartering ships would have required appropriate financial provision and also Ministerial agreement to acknowledge such measures publicly, and this could have been seen as a form of pressure on the Islanders. As it turned out, the inability to give more substance to these civil plans did not matter, as Argentina did not escalate the dispute in the way expected. On the military side the absence of detailed contingency plans for responding to aggressive action by Argentina did not inhibit a very swift response once it was clear that an invasion was imminent, as can be seen from the remarkable speed with which the task force was prepared and sailed. We discuss in paragraphs 324–332 the separate question whether earlier military steps should have been taken to deter an Argentine attack.

Foreign and Commonwealth Office judgment on how the dispute would develop

296. We believe that the view taken by Foreign and Commonwealth Office Ministers and officials early in 1982 of how the dispute would

develop was one which could reasonably be taken in the light of all the circumstances at that time. In the event it proved to be a misjudgment, but not one in our view for which blame should be attached to any individual. There were, we believe, three important factors in the misjudgment: first, in underestimating the importance that Argentina attached to its timetable for resolving the dispute by the end of the year; secondly, in being unduly influenced—understandably and perhaps inevitably—by the long history of the dispute, in which Argentina had previously made threatening noises, accompanied by bellicose press comment, and indeed backed up its threats with aggressive actions, without the dispute developing into a serious confrontation; and, thirdly, in believing, on the basis of evidence, that Argentina would follow an orderly progression in escalating the dispute, starting with economic and diplomatic measures. Sufficient allowance was not made for the possibility of Argentina's military government, subject to internal political and economic pressures, acting unpredictably if at any time they became frustrated at the course of negotiations. The July 1981 intelligence assessment had warned that in those circumstances there was a high risk that Argentina would resort to more forcible measures swiftly and without warning.

The response to events following the New York talks

297. We acknowledge the skill with which Mr. Luce and Foreign and Commonwealth Office officials handled the formal talks between the Argentine and British Governments in New York on 26 and 27 February (see paragraph 133). The agenda for the talks was provided by the Argentine *bout de papier* issued on 27 January. They were held in a cordial atmosphere, and the general view of the British side was that they had gone somewhat better than they feared. A joint *communiqué* was agreed, and in the draft working paper on the negotiating commission reference to the frequency of meetings—an important element in the Argentine proposals—was avoided. At the same time, it had been clear even at the talks that the Argentine side's ability to manoeuvre was strictly limited. The Argentine Government were committed to the establishment of the commission, with negotiations being conducted at high level, at a much faster pace than in the past, and with a strict deadline of a year. They pressed strongly for a formal reply from the British Government to their proposal within a month, with a view to the first round of talks being held at the beginning of April.

298. The unilateral *communiqué* of 1 March instigated by the Junta marked an important change of attitude on the part of the Argentine Government. It in effect denounced the joint *communiqué* by making public the details of the informal working paper, and commended the proposals in the *bout de papier* for a programme of monthly meetings with the aim of achieving recognition of Argentine sovereignty within a short time; and, if those proposals were not effective, claimed the right to choose " the procedure which best accords with [Argentine] interests ". Although Sr. Ros expressed regret about the *communiqué* and accompanying press comment, and Dr. Costa Mendez assured the British Ambassador in Buenos Aires that no threat was intended, it indicated a hardening attitude on the part of the Argentine Government, and a commitment to the negotiating commission proposals and the timetable for its work.

299. The increased seriousness of the situation was recognised by Foreign and Commonwealth Office officials. As described in paragraphs 147 and 148, they discussed it with Lord Carrington at a short meeting on 5 March, at which several diplomatic initiatives were set in hand.

300. This was also the occasion when they mentioned to him the previous Government's decision in November 1977 to deploy ships to the area covertly, though without recommending similar action at that stage. As it happens, 5 March was about the last moment at which, given that the invasion took place on 2 April, it would have been possible to sail a deterrent force to be in place in time. It would have taken nuclear-powered submarines approximately two weeks and surface ships approximately three weeks to reach the Falkland Islands. The evidence we received suggested to us that Foreign and Commonwealth Office officials did not press Ministers to consider deterrent rather than diplomatic counter-measures or prompt the Joint Intelligence Organisation urgently to update its July 1981 assessment because they believed that Argentina would not resort to military action before initiating diplomatic and economic measures.

301. Officials were also looking for an early meeting of the Defence Committee, which Lord Carrington had envisaged taking place after the February talks, and it was expected that the meeting would take place on 16 March. No paper was tabled for that meeting, however, because Lord Carrington thought it right to await the Argentine Government's reaction to the message he was proposing to send to Dr. Costa Mendez.

302. We believe that Foreign and Commonwealth Office officials did not attach sufficient weight at this time to the changing Argentine attitude at and following the February talks and did not give sufficient importance to the new and threatening elements in the Argentine Government's position. We conclude that they should have drawn Ministers' attention more effectively to the changed situation.

303. We note that the Prime Minister reacted to the telegrams from the British Ambassador in Buenos Aires on 3 March reporting aggressive Argentine press comment following the New York talks, and called for contingency plans (see paragraph 152). We regret that the Prime Minister's enquiries did not receive a prompt response. She also enquired of Mr. Nott on 8 March about the timing of possible warship movements to the South Atlantic (see paragraph 153).

The Joint Intelligence Organisation

304. The reports by the intelligence agencies and the assessments made by the Joint Intelligence Committee were a key factor in the judgments made by Ministers and officials in the period leading up to the invasion, which we have reviewed above. A description of the structure and role of the Joint Intelligence Organisation is contained in Annex B. For many years Argentina and the Falkland Islands were regarded as a priority for intelligence collection but were in a relatively low category.

Earlier intelligence assessments

305. From 1965 the Argentine threat to the Falkland Islands was regularly assessed by the Joint Intelligence Committee, the frequency of assessment increasing at times of heightened tension between Britain and

Argentina in the dispute on sovereignty, in the light of the internal political situation in Argentina and information about Argentine intentions. The timing of assessments was often related to the rounds of formal negotiations between the British and Argentine Governments. In the period of the present Government a full assessment was prepared in November 1979, which we summarised in paragraph 77.

The assessment of July 1981

306. A further full assessment, the last before the invasion, was prepared in July 1981. We summarised its contents in paragraphs 94–95. This assessment was particularly important because, as was apparent from the oral evidence we received, it had considerable influence on the thinking of Ministers and officials.

Review of the 1981 assessment

307. We were told in evidence that the Latin America Current Intelligence Group met 18 times between July 1981 and March 1982, but did not discuss the Falkland Islands on those occasions. They were, however, discussed on two occasions in that period at the weekly meetings held by the Head of the assessments staff; and on at least four separate occasions consideration was given by those concerned, who were in close touch with the Foreign and Commonwealth Office on this matter, to the need to update the assessment made in July 1981. These occasions were in November 1981, in preparation for the next round of talks, which were then scheduled for the following month; in December 1981; in January 1982, in the light of the proposals that it was known that Argentina would put forward before the February talks in New York; and in March 1982. On each occasion up to March it was decided that there was no need to revise the assessment.

308. We were told that the four principal factors that the assessments staff considered in assessing the Argentine threat were: the progress of Argentina's dispute with Chile over the Beagle Channel; the political and economic situation in Argentina; the state of inter-service rivalry there; and, most importantly, Argentina's perception of the prospects of making progress by negotiation. The information they received after July 1981 was not thought to indicate any significant change in these factors which would have justified a new assessment. The conclusions reached in July 1981 about Argentine intentions and the options open to them were regarded as consistent with more recent intelligence and therefore still valid.

309. In March 1982 it was agreed that a new assessment should be prepared, and work was started on it. It was thought, however, that it could most usefully be presented to Ministers in the context of a more general consideration of Falkland Islands policy, which they were expected to discuss at a meeting of the Defence Committee on 16 March. In the event, as we have explained, that meeting did not take place, and the new assessment was never completed.

310. The next assessment, which we described in paragraph 230, was made at very short notice in the morning of 31 March and was concerned with events on South Georgia. In its conclusion it expressed the view that, while the possibility that Argentina might choose to escalate the situation

by landing a military force on another Dependency or on the Falkland Islands could not be ruled out, the Argentine Government did not wish to be the first to adopt forcible measures.

The intelligence agencies

311. This assessment on the eve of the invasion relied chiefly on the information available from the intelligence agencies, whose role and relationship with Government Departments and the Joint Intelligence Organisation are described in Annex B. Throughout the period leading up to the invasion secret intelligence was collected, in accordance with the priority accorded to this target, on Argentina's attitude to and intentions in the dispute, in particular the views of its armed forces and Ministry of Foreign Affairs; on relevant internal factors in Argentina; and on its general military capability. In October 1981, following a general review of intelligence requirements in Central and South America and the Caribbean, the Joint Intelligence Committee notified the collecting agencies that, in view of the increasing difficulty of maintaining negotiations with Argentina over the future of the Falkland Islands, the requirement had increased for intelligence on Argentine intentions and policies on the issue. But additional resources were not allocated for this purpose. We were told in evidence that, for operational reasons which were explained to us, the deployment of additional resources would not necessarily have secured earlier or better intelligence of the intentions of the very small circle at the head of the Argentine Government where decisions were taken.

312. If, as we believe, the decision to invade was taken by the Junta at a very late stage, the intelligence agencies could not have been expected to provide earlier warning of the actual invasion on 2 April. It might have been possible to give some warning of the military preparations preceding the invasion, if there had been direct coverage of military movements within Argentina in addition to coverage of its general military capability. But it would have been difficult to provide comprehensive coverage of these movements in view of, among other things, Argentina's very long coastline and the distance of the southern Argentine ports from Buenos Aires. The British Defence *Attaché* in Buenos Aires told us that his section at the Embassy had neither the remit nor the capacity to obtain detailed information of this kind. By the time the diplomatic situation deteriorated at the beginning of March it would have been difficult to evaluate such information because of the absence of knowledge about the normal pattern of Argentine military activity.

313. There was no coverage of Argentine military movements within Argentina, and no advance information was therefore available by these means about the composition and assembly of the Argentine naval force that eventually invaded the Falklands. There was no intelligence from American sources or otherwise to show that the force at sea before the invasion was intended other than for normal naval exercises. No satellite photography was available on the disposition of the Argentine forces. The British Naval *Attaché* in Buenos Aires reported the naval exercises when he became aware of them, mainly on the basis of Argentine press reports.

314. We have no reason to question the reliability of the intelligence that was regularly received from a variety of sources.

Did the intelligence assessment machinery function effectively?

315. As to assessments, however, we were surprised that events in the first three months of 1982, in particular the Argentine *bout de papier* on 27 January, the unilateral *communiqué* on 1 March and the Prime Minister's comments on the telegram of 3 March reporting Argentine press comment, did not prompt the Joint Intelligence Organisation to assess the situation afresh. As we have explained, the assessments staff considered the need for a new assessment on several occasions in this period. Work was started on one early in March, but not completed because of the intention to link it to a meeting of the Defence Committee. It was decided not to prepare a new assessment before the beginning of March because of the view in the Joint Intelligence Organisation that the conclusions of a new assessment were unlikely to be significantly different from those of the July 1981 assessment. The assessment of 31 March 1982, although focused on the South Georgia incident, tends to support this view.

316. We do not regard the view taken by those concerned of the need for a new assessment as unreasonable in the light of the information available to them at the time. But in our consideration of the evidence we remain doubtful about two aspects of the work of the Joint Intelligence Organisation. First, we are not sure that at all important times the assessments staff were fully aware of the weight of the Argentine press campaign in 1982. As a result it seems to us that they may have attached greater significance to the secret intelligence, which at that time was reassuring about the prospects of an early move to confrontation. For instance, the intelligence referred to in paragraph 131 pointed out that the press campaign was probably designed to exert pressure on the United Kingdom in the negotiations. Our second doubt is whether the Joint Intelligence Organisation attached sufficient weight to the possible effects on Argentine thinking of the various actions of the British Government. The changes in the Argentine position were, we believe, more evident on the diplomatic front and in the associated press campaign than in the intelligence reports.

317. We do not seek to attach any blame to the individuals involved. But we believe that these factors point to the need for a clearer understanding of the relative roles of the assessments staff, the Foreign and Commonwealth Office and the Ministry of Defence, and for closer liaison between them. The aim should be to ensure that the assessments staff are able to take fully into account both relevant diplomatic and political developments and foreign press treatment of sensitive foreign policy issues.

318. We are concerned here with defects in the Joint Intelligence machinery as we have seen it working in an area of low priority. As we have seen only the papers relevant to the subject of our review, we are not able to judge how the assessment machinery deals with areas of higher priority, but we believe that, in dealing with Argentina and the Falkland Islands it was too passive in operation to respond quickly and critically to a rapidly changing situation which demanded urgent attention.

319. We consider that the assessment machinery should be reviewed. We cannot say what the scope of such a review should be in respect of the machinery's wider preoccupations, but we think that it should look at two aspects in particular. The first, to which we have already referred, is the arrangements for bringing to the Joint Intelligence Organisation's

attention information other than intelligence reports. The second is the composition of the Joint Intelligence Committee. On this, consideration should be given to the position of the chairman of the Committee: to the desirability that he or she should be full-time, with a more critical and independent role; and, in recognition of the Committee's independence in operation from the Government Departments principally constituting it, to the Chairman's being appointed by the Prime Minister and being a member of the Cabinet Office.

320. The suggestions we have made about the Joint Intelligence Organisation derive only from our consideration of the Falkland Islands issue. We put these suggestions forward as a guide for the future. Any view of the effect they might have had on the period we have studied would be hypothetical and speculative.

Impact of the South Georgia incident

321. If the Joint Intelligence Committee machinery had operated differently, we have no reason to believe that it would have increased the intelligence available to the Government about the operations of Sr. Davidoff, which led to the South Georgia incident preceding the invasion. There are still uncertainties about the full scope and character of those operations. The visits to South Georgia, by Sr. Davidoff himself in December 1981 and by his party in March 1982, were both made on Argentine naval vessels, and the Argentine Navy was no doubt aware of them. But there was no evidence at the time, and none has come to light since, suggesting that the whole operation was planned either by the Argentine Government or by the Navy as a follow-up to the occupation of Southern Thule. The intelligence available indicates that, when the incident grew more serious it was seized on to escalate the situation until the Junta finally decided to invade the Falkland Islands.

322. We recognise that the response of Ministers had to take account of conflicting pressures at home, especially from Parliament, and from Argentina. The initial reports of the incident appeared alarming—shots having been fired and the Argentine flag run up—and it was a reasonable reaction to order *HMS Endurance* to sail to South Georgia to take the men off. Thereafter the Government went to great lengths to avoid exacerbating the situation and made every effort to offer constructive ways of enabling the Argentine party to regularise its position. These were all rejected by the Argentine Government, which by then were clearly intent on raising the temperature.

323. Nevertheless we believe that, if Sr. Davidoff's operations had been more closely monitored from December 1981 onwards and there had been better liaison between the Foreign and Commonwealth Office, the British Embassy in Buenos Aires and the Governor in preparation for the second visit in March 1982, Ministers would have been better able to deal with the landing on South Georgia when it occurred.

The possibility of earlier deterrent action

324. We next examine whether the Government should have taken earlier military action to deter Argentina. We have considered two possible actions that the Government might have taken: the earlier despatch of a task force on a sufficient scale to defend, or if necessary retake, the

Islands; and the deployment of a much smaller force in the form of a nuclear-powered submarine, either on its own or supported by surface ships.

325. We believe that it would not have been appropriate to prepare a large task force with the capacity to retake the Falkland Islands, before there was clear evidence of an invasion. As we have explained, this was not perceived to be imminent until 31 March. Sending such a force would have been a disproportionate, and indeed provocative, response to the events on South Georgia, and would have been inconsistent with the attempts being made to resolve the problems there by diplomatic means.

326. A smaller force might have been deployed, either overtly as a deterrent measure or covertly as a precautionary measure, whose existence could have been declared if circumstances required. There were three occasions when such a force might reasonably have been deployed: before the New York talks at the end of February; at the beginning of March in the light of evidence of increased Argentine impatience at lack of progress in negotiations; or later in March, as events on South Georgia moved towards confrontation.

327. In this connection parallels have been drawn with the action taken by the previous Government in November 1977, when two frigates and a nuclear-powered submarine were deployed to the area. On that occasion the deployment was made covertly to buttress negotiations. The closest parallel is therefore with the talks in New York in February 1982. At that time there were signs of growing Argentine impatience, in the form of the *bout de papier* and the accompanying hostile press comment in Argentina, but in other respects the circumstances were different from those obtaining at the time of the 1977 talks. 1977 was a tense period in Anglo-Argentine relations and there was a sharper risk of Argentine military action. Ambassadors had been withdrawn at the beginning of the previous year; there had been a much more recent infringement of British sovereignty in the form of the establishment of an Argentine presence on Southern Thule; and there had been physical acts of aggression by Argentina against foreign shipping. Before the talks in 1977 the Joint Intelligence Committee assessed that, if negotiations broke down, there would be a high risk of Argentina's resorting to more forceful measures; in those circumstances action against British shipping was seen as the most serious risk.

328. It was believed that the round of talks in December 1977 could lead to a breakdown of negotiations. The circumstances leading up to the February 1982 talks were different, and we consider that they did not warrant a similar naval deployment.

329. There was a stronger case for considering action of this nature early in March 1982, in the light of evidence of increasing Argentine impatience, culminating in the threatening *communiqué* issued on 1 March by the Argentine Ministry of Foreign Affairs and the accompanying bellicose Argentine press comment. As we explained in paragraph 148, Lord Carrington was informed of the action taken in 1977 at the end of a short meeting on 5 March. Lord Carrington told us in oral evidence that the matter was mentioned only briefly. He asked whether the Argentines knew about the naval deployment, and, when told that they did not, he took the view that this reduced its relevance to the situation he faced. Lord Carrington

also told us more generally that, although the situation had become more difficult, he did not believe that the prospect of continuing negotiations at that time was hopeless. In his view nothing had happened to trigger the sending of a deterrent force. He was concerned that, if ships were sent, the fact would have become known. This would have jeopardised the prospect of keeping negotiations going, which was his objective. With hindsight he wished he had sought to deploy a nuclear-powered submarine to the area at an earlier stage, but on 5 March it did not seem to him that the situation had changed in such a way as to justify such action.

330.   We do not think that this was an unreasonable view to take at the time, but we believe that there would have been advantage in the Government's giving wider consideration at this stage to the question whether the potentially more threatening attitude by Argentina required some form of deterrent action in addition to the diplomatic initiatives and the contingency planning already in hand.

331.   Finally, we consider whether earlier action should have been taken to deploy ships to the area in response to the developing crisis on South Georgia. In Lord Carrington's judgment a deployment involving surface ships was likely to carry too great a risk of becoming known at a time when the Government were concerned to avoid any action that might have appeared provocative. That could have provoked escalatory action by Argentina against the Falkland Islands themselves, which the Government had no means of resisting effectively. This objection would not have applied so strongly to sailing a nuclear-powered submarine, since there would have been more chance of keeping its deployment covert. The decision to sail the first nuclear-powered submarine was taken early on Monday 29 March.

332.   We consider that there was a case for taking this action at the end of the previous week in the light of the telegram of 24 March from the Defence *Attaché* in Buenos Aires (see paragraph 192) and the report of 25 March that Argentine ships had been sailed for a possible interception of *HMS Endurance*. We would have expected a quicker reaction in the Ministry of Defence to these two reports, which were the first indications of hostile activity by the Argentine Government.

Final warnings to Argentina

333.   The British Government took several opportunities in the weeks leading up to the invasion to state publicly their commitment to the defence of the Falkland Islands and the Dependencies. In the House of Commons on 23 March Mr. Luce stated that it was the " duty of this Government and of any British Government to defend and support the Islanders to the best of their ability ".(¹) On 25 March the British Ambassador in Buenos Aires, on instructions, warned Dr. Costa Mendez that Britain was committed to the defence of its sovereignty in South Georgia as elsewhere. As soon as a threat to the Falkland Islands themselves was perceived, the Prime Minister contacted President Reagan on 31 March and asked him to make it clear to the Argentine Government that the Government could not acquiesce in action against the Falkland Islands. As the Prime Minister explained to us in evidence, without the collective advice of the Chiefs of

(¹) *Official Report*, House of Commons, 23 March 1982, Col. 799.

Staff on whether an operation to retake the Islands was feasible and the approval of Cabinet, it was not possible for her to go further. In the event, when speaking personally to General Galtieri, President Reagan stated forcefully that action against the Falklands would be regarded by the British as a *casus belli*.

334. We conclude that warnings by the British Government of the consequences of invading the Falkland Islands were conveyed to the Argentine Government.

Could the present Government have prevented the invasion of 2 April 1982 ?

335. Finally we turn to the more complex question we posed in the opening paragraph of this Chapter. Could the present Government have prevented the invasion of 2 April 1982?

336. It is a question that has to be considered in the context of the period of 17 years covered by our Report: there is no simple answer to it. We have given a detailed factual account of the period, and we attach special importance to our account of events immediately preceding the invasion. It is essential that our Report should be read as a whole—and to recognise, as we do, that there were deep roots to Argentina's attitude towards the ' Malvinas ', and that the present Government had to deal with that within the political constraints accepted by successive British Governments.

337. As to the Argentine Government—and this is quite apart from the influence on the Argentine Government of actions of the British Government—the Junta was confronted at the end of March 1982 with a rapidly deteriorating economic situation and strong political pressures at a moment when it was able to exploit to its advantage the developments in South Georgia. We have already stated at the beginning of this Chapter the reasons why we are convinced that the invasion on 2 April 1982 could not have been foreseen.

338. The British Government, on the other hand, had to act within the constraints imposed by the wishes of the Falkland Islanders, which had a moral force of their own as well as the political support of an influential body of Parliamentary opinion; and also by strategic and military priorities which reflected national defence and economic policies: Britain's room for policy manoeuvre was limited.

339. Against this background we have pointed out in this Chapter where different decisions might have been taken, where fuller consideration of alternative courses of action might, in our opinion, have been advantageous, and where the machinery of Government could have been better used. But, if the British Government had acted differently in the ways we have indicated, it is impossible to judge what the impact on the Argentine Government or the implications for the course of events might have been. There is no reasonable basis for any suggestion—which would be purely hypothetical—that the invasion would have been prevented if the Government had acted in the ways indicated in our report. Taking account of these considerations, and of all the evidence we have received,

we conclude that we would not be justified in attaching any criticism or blame to the present Government for the Argentine Junta's decision to commit its act of unprovoked aggression in the invasion of the Falkland Islands on 2 April 1982.

FRANKS, *Chairman*

BARBER

LEVER

PATRICK NAIRNE

MERLYN REES

WATKINSON

A. R. RAWSTHORNE, *Secretary*

P. G. MOULSON, *Assistant Secretary*

31st December, 1982

COMMENTS ON SOME SPECIFIC ASSERTIONS

There has understandably been much speculation about the causes of the Falkland Islands conflict and about whether it could have been foreseen and prevented. The truth of these matters is less simple than some commentators have asserted, and for an accurate and comprehensive account of the facts our Report needs to be read in full. In the detailed narrative of events and our comments on them we have answered explicitly or by implication many of the mistaken or misleading statements that have been made, but we think it right also to state for the record our view of some of the more important specific assertions which have been made, in order to clear up damaging misunderstandings.

1. *Assertion:* Ministers and officials secretly told Argentina that Britain was prepared to give up the Falkland Islands against the wishes of the Islanders.

   Comment: We have found no evidence to support this allegation. On the contrary, Ministers and officials made clear to Argentina on numerous occasions that the wishes of the Falkland Islanders were paramount, and that any proposals to resolve the dispute would be subject to approval by Parliament.

2. *Assertion:* Clear warnings of the invasion from American intelligence sources were circulating more than a week beforehand.

   Comment: No intelligence about the invasion was received from American sources, before it took place, by satellite or otherwise.

3. *Assertion:* On or around 24 March 1982 the British Embassy in Buenos Aires passed on definite information to London about an invasion and predicted the exact day.

   Comment: This assertion derives from newspaper interviews after the invasion. We have investigated these interviews. It is not our task to come to any conclusion about what was or was not said to the journalists concerned or whether or not what was said was correctly interpreted. It is our task, however, to ascertain beyond doubt whether any such communication from the British Embassy in Buenos Aires predicting the invasion was in fact made. We have examined all the relevant telegrams and intelligence reports and interviewed the individuals concerned. We are satisfied that no such communication was in fact made.

4. *Assertions:* (i) Two weeks before the invasion the Cabinet's Defence Committee rejected a proposal by Lord Carrington to send submarines to the area;

   (ii) The Government rejected advice from the Commander-in-Chief, Fleet, to send submarines soon after the landing on South Georgia on 19 March.

   Comment: These assertions are untrue. We have described in detail the events of the weeks leading up to the invasion. The Defence Committee did not meet at that time. The first discussion between Ministers about sending nuclear-powered submarines took place on Monday 29 March 1982 when the Prime Minister and Lord Carrington decided that a nuclear-powered submarine should be sent to support *HMS Endurance*. No earlier military advice recommending the despatch of submarines was given to Ministers.

5. *Assertion:* Argentina was informed by the British Government of their decision to send a task force in 1977.

   Comment: The facts relating to the deployment of ships to the area in November 1977 are set out in our Report (see paragraphs 65–66). We have had no evidence that the Argentine Government became aware of this deployment.

6. *Assertions:* (i) Captain Barker, the Captain of *HMS Endurance*, sent warnings that an invasion was imminent which were ignored by the Foreign and Commonwealth Office and the Ministry of Defence.

(ii) The Secretary of State for Defence saw Captain Barker and ignored his advice.

Comment: These assertions are untrue. Captain Barker reported his concern about events within his knowledge, but none of his reports warned of an imminent invasion. Both the Ministry of Defence and the Foreign and Commonwealth Office saw his reports and took them into account along with other intelligence material. Captain Barker confirmed to us that he never met Mr. Nott.

7. *Assertion:* On 11 March 1982 an Argentine military plane landed at Port Stanley to reconnoitre the runway. The incident was reported by the Governor as suspicious.

Comment: The emergency landing on 7 March of an Argentine Air Force Hercules transport aircraft was reported factually by the Governor to the Foreign and Commonwealth Office on 12 March but not as suspicious. He has subsequently confirmed that the landing was preceded by a ' May Day ' call and that, after the aircraft landed, fuel was seen leaking from it. The Argentine Air Force would already have had detailed knowledge of the strength of the runway in consequence of its responsibility for operating the flights between Port Stanley and Argentina and of authorised landings by Argentine Hercules aircraft at Port Stanley on several occasions in 1981.

8. *Assertion:* The Argentine Government made a bulk purchase of maps of the Falkland Islands in Britain before the invasion.

Comment: An investigation by the Foreign and Commonwealth Office found that no such bulk purchase was made. This has been confirmed by the agents for the sale of the hydrographic charts produced by the Royal Navy. It has also been confirmed by the agents for the sale of the 1966 map of the Falkland Islands published by the Directorate of Overseas Surveys, copies of which were left on the Islands by the Argentine forces.

9. *Assertion:* There were massive withdrawals of Argentine funds from London banks shortly before the invasion, of which the Government must have been aware.

Comment: We are satisfied that the Government had no information about such a movement of funds. The deposit liabilities of United Kingdom banks to overseas countries are reported to the Bank of England on a quarterly basis. The reporting date relevant to the period before the invasion was 31 March 1982, but, because of the complexity of the figures, they normally take several weeks to collect. Withdrawals by Argentine banks in March would therefore not have normally been reported until May. After the invasion the Bank of England asked banks for a special report, and this showed that around $\frac{1}{2}$ billion of the original $1\frac{1}{2}$ billion of Argentine funds were moved out of London in the period running up to the invasion, much of it on 1 and 2 April. Since the withdrawals were in dollars, there would have been no effect on the sterling exchange rate to alert the Bank of England.

10. *Assertion:* On 29 March 1982 the Uruguayan Government offered the British Government facilities for Falkland Islanders who wished to leave the Islands before the Argentine invasion.

Comment: Neither the Foreign and Commonwealth Office nor the British Embassy in Montevideo had knowledge at the time or thereafter of any such offer. The Uruguayan Government have also described this allegation as completely without foundation. They have confirmed that neither they nor their Navy had any foreknowledge of the Argentine invasion of the Falkland Islands.

ASPECTS OF THE MACHINERY OF GOVERNMENT IN RELATION TO THE FALKLAND ISLANDS

In this Annex we describe briefly the main aspects of the machinery of Government relevant to their responsibilities for the Falkland Islands and the Falkland Islands Dependencies.

The machinery for collective Ministerial consideration and decision

2.   Collective Ministerial decisions are taken by the Cabinet and Cabinet Committees.   The standing committee of the Cabinet for discussing and deciding foreign policy and defence issues is the Defence and Oversea Policy Committee (to which, for the sake of brevity, we refer as the ' Defence Committee ').   The Defence Committee is chaired by the Prime Minister.   Its membership includes the Secretaries of State for Foreign and Commonwealth Affairs and for Defence and the Chancellor of the Exchequer.   The Chiefs of Staff are in attendance as required, to tender professional military advice.   The timing and agenda of meetings of the Defence Committee are ultimately a matter for the Prime Minister, advised by the Secretary of the Cabinet and the Cabinet Secretariat.   Meetings are arranged as required.

Foreign and Commonwealth Office

3.   The Ministerial head of the Foreign and Commonwealth Office is the Secretary of State for Foreign and Commonwealth Affairs.   Lord Carrington was the Foreign and Commonwealth Secretary from the time the present Government took office in May 1979 until his resignation on 5 April 1982.   The Foreign and Commonwealth Secretary is assisted by a team of Ministers, to whom he assigns responsibility under his overall direction for specific subjects and matters relating to different parts of the world.   While Lord Carrington was Foreign and Commonwealth Secretary, the second most senior Minister in the Foreign and Commonwealth Office was the Lord Privy Seal, who was also a member of the Cabinet.   Sir Ian Gilmour, M P was Lord Privy Seal from May 1979 to September 1981 and Mr. Humphrey Atkins, M P from September 1981 until his resignation on 5 April 1982.   In addition to his other responsibilities, which did not include matters relating to Argentina or the Falkland Islands, Mr. Atkins had a particular responsibility for matters with a significant Parliamentary aspect.   Matters relating to Argentina and the Falkland Islands, among many other areas in the world, were the responsibility of one of the Ministers of State, from May 1979 to September 1981 Mr. Nicholas Ridley, M P and from September 1981 to his resignation on 5 April 1982 Mr. Richard Luce, M P.   Formal negotiations at ministerial level with the Argentine Government about the Falkland Islands were generally conducted by the Minister of State.

4.   The permanent head of the Foreign and Commonwealth Office and Head of the Diplomatic Service is the Permanent Under-Secretary of State, from 1975 until his retirement in April 1982 Sir Michael Palliser.   The Office has departments principally organised on a geographical basis, each department being headed by an official of Counsellor rank (equivalent to an Assistant Secretary in the Home Civil Service).   At the time of the invasion the relevant department for Falkland Islands matters was the South America Department, which was also responsible for relations with all the countries in South America.   It had been headed since November 1979 by Mr. P. R. Fearn.   The work of this Department was under the supervision of a Superintending Assistant Under-Secretary of State, from January 1981 Mr. J. B. Ure, who also supervised the North America, the West Indian and Atlantic, the Mexico and Central America and (in part) the Hong Kong and General Departments.   He in turn was responsible to the Permanent Under-Secretary of State through a Deputy Under-Secretary of State, from February 1980 until February 1982 Mr. D. M. Day, and from March 1982 Mr. S. Giffard.

5. In Argentina, the British Government were represented by the British Ambassador in Buenos Aires and his staff. Mr. A. J. Williams was British Ambassador from February 1980 until April 1982. The Defence *Attaché* in Buenos Aires was Colonel S. Love and the Naval *Attaché* Captain J. J. Mitchell, R N. The *Attachés* were seconded to the British Embassy from the Ministry of Defence.

Government of the Falkland Islands and Dependencies

6. Her Majesty's Government are responsible for the government and defence of the Falkland Islands and for external relations in respect of them. The Falkland Islands have a constitution, granted by the British Government, under which they have their own government and legislature.

7. In the period before the invasion, under the constitution, the Governor of the Falkland Islands, from February 1979 Mr. R. M. Hunt (now Sir Rex Hunt), was subject to the directions of the Crown given through the Secretary of State. The Governor had full reserve executive and legislative powers, but in practice these powers were very rarely exercised. He was also Commander-in-Chief.

8. The Governor was assisted in the administration of Government by an Executive Council composed of two elected members, two *ex officio* members (the Chief Secretary and the Financial Secretary) and two members nominated by the Governor. The Legislative Council was composed of six elected and two *ex officio* members (the Chief Secretary and the Financial Secretary).

9. The Falkland Islands Dependencies are not part of the colony of the Falkland Islands, but constitute a separate colony. The Governor of the Falkland Islands and the Executive Council were also the Governor and Executive Council of the Dependencies.

Ministry of Defence

10. The ministerial head of the Ministry of Defence is the Secretary of State for Defence, from January 1981 Mr. John Nott, M P. He is assisted by two Ministers of State, one for the Armed Forces and one for Defence Procurement, and two Parliamentary Under-Secretaries of State. The Minister of State and the Parliamentary Under-Secretary of State for the Armed Forces at the time of the invasion were Mr. Peter Blaker, M P and Mr. Jerry Wiggin, M P respectively.

11. The principal military adviser to the Government is the Chief of the Defence Staff, who is Chairman of the Chiefs of Staff Committee. The Chief of the Defence Staff has a right of direct access to the Prime Minister. The Service Chiefs of Staff (the Chief of the Naval Staff, the Chief of the General Staff and the Chief of the Air Staff) are the senior military advisers to the Government on matters concerning their own Services. They have a right of direct access to the Prime Minister on these matters. At the time of the invasion Admiral Sir Terence Lewin (now Lord Lewin) was Chief of the Defence Staff, Admiral Sir Henry Leach Chief of the Naval Staff, General Sir Edwin Bramall Chief of the General Staff, and Air Chief Marshal Sir Michael Beetham Chief of the Air Staff.

12. The principal adviser to the Defence Secretary on political, financial and administrative matters is the Permanent Under-Secretary of State, from March 1976 Sir Frank Cooper. The Defence Secretariat is responsible for advising him, and through him the Defence Secretary, on the Defence programme and budget and the political background associated with Defence policy, including overseas matters, in consultation with the Foreign and Commonwealth Office.

Joint Intelligence Organisation

13. The Joint Intelligence Organisation is an organisation based in the Cabinet Office which is responsible for making assessments for Ministers and officials of a wide range of external situations and developments. It draws for its assessments on

94

all relevant information: diplomatic reports and telegrams, the views of Government departments and publicly available information, as well as secret intelligence reports. It also has a co-ordinating role in respect of the work of the security and intelligence agencies.

14. Assessments are normally considered before circulation by the Joint Intelligence Committee. The Joint Intelligence Committee is normally chaired by a Deputy Under-Secretary of State in the Foreign and Commonwealth Office. Its members include representatives of the security and intelligence agencies, the Foreign and Commonwealth Office, the Ministry of Defence and the Treasury.

15. Assessments are prepared for consideration by the Joint Intelligence Committee by Current Intelligence Groups, which are serviced by the Assessments Staff, who are civil servants and serving officers seconded to the Cabinet Office from their own Departments, principally the Foreign and Commonwealth Office and the Ministry of Defence. The Current Intelligence Groups are organised on a geographical basis. There is one for Latin America. Their membership is drawn from those in the relevant Departments with special knowledge of the area. They are chaired by members of the Assessments Staff. Assessments are prepared at the instigation of Ministers, of Departments or of the Joint Intelligence Organisation itself.

Security and intelligence agencies

16. The collection, but not the assessment, of secret intelligence is the responsibility of the security and intelligence agencies. On operational matters relevant to the subject of our review the agencies report to the Foreign and Commonwealth Office, but they serve the Government as a whole and their heads have a right of direct access to the Prime Minister. Their reports are circulated to, among others, the Foreign and Commonwealth Office and the Ministry of Defence as well as to the Joint Intelligence Organisation.

PERSONS AND ORGANISATIONS FROM WHOM WRITTEN SUBMISSIONS WERE RECEIVED

The Rt. Hon. Julian Amery, M P
Sir Bernard Braine, D L, M P
Mr. Tam Dalyell, M P
Mr. Michael English, M P
Mr. Eldon Griffiths, M A, M P
Sir Geoffrey Johnson Smith M P
Mr. Robin Maxwell-Hyslop, M P
The Rt. Hon. Dr. David Owen, M P
Mr. Roger Sims, J P, M P
Mr. Keith Stainton, M P
Dr. the Hon. Shirley Summerskill, M P
Mr. Peter Temple-Morris, M P
Mr. Neville Trotter, F C A, J P, M P

Lord Bethell, M E P
Lt.-Col. The Lord Burnham
Lord Buxton of Alsa, M C, D L
Lord Kennet
Lord Swann, F R S

Mr. R. D. J. Arnold

Mr. T. A. Bacon
Sir Roderick Barclay, G C V O, K C M G
Mr. A. G. Barker
Dr. P. Beck
Mr. J. D. Berridge
Mr. G. V. M. Bird
Mr. H. J. Birkett
Mr. A. Birnie
Miss M. Blacoe
Dr. H. Blakemore
Mr. W. Bowden
Mr. T. W. Boyd Junior, M A
The British Antarctic Survey
Mr. M. Brown
Mr. J. R. Bryans
Mr. B. Bufton

Captain E. P. Carlisle
Mr. R. Carr
Sir Roger Cary, Bart
Mr. N. Charlton
Mr. A. Charnaud
Mr. S. Chesine
Mr. A. W. Craig
Mr. P. Crane
Ms. D. Crisp
Mr. J. Crompton

Mr. W. R. Dalton
Mr. G. Davies
Captain J. C. Davies
Mr. D. Delderfield
Mr. A. J. Dixon
Mr. D. Dixon
Mr. H. Dowson

Mr. S. Ebdale

Mr. O. Fordham

Vice-Admiral Sir John Gray, K B E, O B E

Mr. A. C. Hall, C B E
Miss J. Hall
Sir Cosmo Haskard, K C M G, M B E
Mr. A. Hoyle
Miss W. D'Leny Huxtable

Mr. D. J. James, M B E, D S C

Mrs. K. E. Keeley
Lt.-Col. D. Kennedy
Mr. R. A. Kennedy
Mr. R. Klaber

Mr. R. D. Leakey
Mr. E. G. Lewis, C M G, O B E
Sir D. Logan, K C M G
Mr. R. M. P. Ludlow

Mr. P. MacBryan
Mr. G. A. Makin
Mr. E. A. Marsh
Mr. M. Mason
Mr. K. R. May

Mr. J. F. Nall
National Union of Seamen
Dr. N. Naunton-Davis
Mr. H. W. Newman
Mrs. M. Nichols

Mr. S. Osborn

Mr. M. Parker
Mr. M. W. Parish
Mr. A. S. Plane
Professor D. C. M. Platt, M A, D Phil
Mr. M. D. Pollard
Dr. F. Pygott

Mr. N. Reddaway, C B E
Mr. F. J. Revell
Mr. H. Riley
Mr. P. Riley
Dr. P. Rodgers
Mr. C. Roper
Mr. J. D. Rudhaver
Mr. O. Russell
Mr. D. Rutherford
Sir Martin Ryle, F R S

Major R. Sanderson
Mr. G. Scutcheon
Mr. L. W. Shaw
Mr. A. Sinclair
Mr. D. G. Smith
The Rev. G. Smith
Mr. L. M. Smith
Mr. G. Squires
Major R. N. Spafford
Mr. K. Standring
Mr. G. Stern
Mr. R. Stone
Mr. R. W. Storey
Miss J. Sykes

Mr. D. Tempest

UK Falkland Islands Committee

Mr. M. Wheeler
Mr. J. Williams
Mr. R. Wilkie
Mr. G. Winkel
Mr. J. Witham

REPLIES RECEIVED FROM NEWSPAPER EDITORS

Replies, other than acknowledgements, to the Committee's request for any specific information in the first three months of 1982 which indicated the possibility of an Argentine invasion of the Falkland Islands were received from:

Cambridge Evening News

Daily Mail

The Guardian

The Observer

The Sunday Times

Sunderland Echo

PERSONS WHO GAVE ORAL EVIDENCE

Ministers and former Ministers of the present Administration

The Prime Minister, the Rt. Hon. Margaret Thatcher, M P
The Rt. Hon. The Lord Carrington, K C M G, M C
The Rt. Hon. John Nott, M P
The Rt. Hon. Humphrey Atkins, M P
Mr. Richard Luce, M P
The Hon. Nicholas Ridley, M P

Former Prime Ministers

The Rt. Hon. Sir Harold Wilson, K G, O B E, F R S, M P
The Rt. Hon. Edward Heath, M B E, M P
The Rt. Hon. James Callaghan, M P

Other Ministers of previous Administrations

The Rt. Hon. Dr. David Owen, M P
Mr. Edward Rowlands, M P

Government Departments

  (i) *Cabinet Office*

    Sir Robert Armstrong, K C B, C V O
    Mr. R. L. L. Facer
    Mr. D. H. Colvin

  (ii) *Foreign and Commonwealth Office*

    Sir Antony Acland, K C M G, K C V O
    Sir Michael Palliser, G C M G
    Mr. D. M. Day, C M G
    Mr. J. B. Ure, C M G, M V O
    Mr. P. R. Fearn
    Mr. A. Williams, C M G
    Mr. M. S. R. Heathcote
    Colonel S. Love, M B E
    Captain J. J. Mitchell, R N
    Sir Rex Hunt, C M G

  (iii) *Ministry of Defence*

    Sir Frank Cooper, G C B, C M G
    Admiral Sir Terence Lewin, G C B, M V O, D S C (now Lord Lewin)
    Admiral Sir Henry Leach, G C B
    Admiral Sir John Fieldhouse, G B E, G C B
    Mr. R. T. Jackling, C B E
    Mr. N. H. Nicholls, C B E
    Captain N. J. Barker, C B E, R N

  (iv) *Members of the intelligence community*

Falkland Islands Legislative Council

Mr. J. Blake
Mr. J. Cheek
Mr. T. J. Peck, M B E, C P M

Members of Parliament

Sir Bernard Braine, D L, M P
Lord Buxton of Alsa, M C, D L
Mr. T. Dalyell, M P
The Rt. Hon. The Lord Shackleton, K G, O B E

Media

Mr. K. Clarke
Mr. D. Nicholas
Mr. P. Thornton
Mr. A. Protheroe, M B E, T D
Mr. S. Winchester

The United Kingdom Falkland Islands Committee

Sir John Barlow
Mr. E. W. H. Christie
Mr. R. Elgood

EXTRACT FROM THE *OFFICIAL REPORT*, HOUSE OF COMMONS,
2 DECEMBER 1980
COLUMNS 195–204

Falkland Islands

The Minister of State, Foreign and Commonwealth Office (Mr. Nicholas Ridley):
With permission, Mr. Speaker, I wish to make a statement on the Falkland Islands.

We have no doubt about our sovereignty over the islands. The Argentines, however, continue to press their claim. The dispute is causing continuing uncertainty, emigration and economic stagnation in the islands. Following my exploratory talks with the Argentines in April, the Government have been considering possible ways of achieving a solution which would be acceptable to all the parties. In this the essential is that we should be guided by the wishes of the islanders themselves.

I therefore visited the islands between 22 and 29 November in order to consult island councillors and subsequently, at their express request, all islanders, on how we should proceed. Various possible bases for seeking a negotiated settlement were discussed. These included both a way of freezing the dispute for a period or exchanging the title of sovereignty against a long lease of the islands back to Her Majesty's Government.

The essential elements of any solution would be that it should preserve British administration, law and way of life for the islanders while releasing the potential of the islands' economy and of their maritime resources, at present blighted by the dispute.

It is for the islanders to advise on which, if any, option should be explored in negotiations with the Argentines. I have asked them to let me have their views in due course. Any eventual settlement would have to be endorsed by the islanders, and by this House.

Mr. Peter Shore (Stepney and Poplar): This is a worrying statement.

Will the Minister confirm that involved here are the rights and future of 1,800 people of British descent in a territory which was originally uninhabited—people who, above all, wish to preserve their present relationship with the United Kingdom? Will he reaffirm that there is no question of proceeding with any proposal contrary to the wishes of the Falkland islanders? Their wishes are surely not just " guidance " to the British Government. Surely they must be of paramount importance. Has he made that absolutely clear to the Argentine Government?

Is not the Minister aware that proposals for a leasing arrangement represent a major weakening of our long-held position on sovereignty in the Falkland Islands, and that to make them in so specific and public a manner is likely only to harden Argentine policy and to undermine the confidence of the Falkland islanders? Will he therefore make it clear that we shall uphold the rights of the islanders to continue to make a genuinely free choice about their future, that we shall not abandon them and that, in spite of all the logistic difficulties, we shall continue to support and sustain them?

Mr. Ridley: The answer to all the right hon. Gentleman's question is " Yes ". There are about 1,800 islanders. I make it clear, as I did in my statement, that we shall do nothing which was not " endorsed " by the islanders. I used that word as well as the word " wishes ". I agree that that is the predominant consideration in this matter. I am sure that equally the right hon. Gentleman will agree that nothing that he might feel, think or do should be allowed to interfere with what the islanders themselves decide. I confirm that our long-standing commitment to their security and economic well-being remains, and I said that in the islands.

101

Sir Bernard Braine (Essex, South-East): Does not my right hon. Friend agree that the option of yielding on sovereignty and leasing back undermines a perfectly valid title in international law?

Secondly, does not he realise that the precedent of Hong Kong, which was taken from China by force, is an insult to Falkland islanders whose ancestors went there more than a century ago and settled peaceably in an uninhabited land?

Thirdly, did my hon. Friend discuss with representatives of the Falkland Islands alternative means of communications, which are perfectly feasible, in order to reduce the islands' total dependence upon the Argentine? Lastly, in view of the fresh anxieties that these talks have caused about the future of the islanders, and bearing in mind that the islanders are wholly British in blood and sentiment, will he give an assurance that the Government will include the Falkland islanders as an exception in the forthcoming British nationality law?

Mr. Ridley: I agree with my hon. Friend that we have a perfectly valid title. There is no question about that in our mind. The question is whether the islanders would prefer to have the dead hand of the dispute removed so that they can not only continue their British way of life but have reasonable prospects of economic expansion. I suggest that that is something upon which they have every right to give their views before we all give ours.

I consulted the islanders on the question of communications, but, of course, in the event of a dispute between ourselves and Argentina becoming more tense, my hon. Friend should realise that it is unlikely that communications could be established with neighbouring countries in South America. The question of British nationality is a matter for my right hon. Friend the Home Secretary.

Mr. Russell Johnston (Inverness): Is the Minister aware that his reception in the Falkland Islands left the islanders' views in no doubt, although it left a considerable doubt about his good intentions? Is he further aware that there is no support at all in the Falkland Islands or in this House for the shameful schemes for getting rid of these islands which have been festering in the Foreign Office for years? Will he take this opportunity to end speculation once and for all by declaring quite clearly that he disowns these schemes and that he will work to improve the economic and political links between the United Kingdom and the Falkland Islands? Surely that is the way to end the emigration about which he talked earlier.

Mr. Ridley: Perhaps I am more aware of the reception that I received in the islands than the hon. Gentleman is. I hope that even those who did not like what I had to say were at least agreed upon my good intentions. I can assure the hon. Gentleman that a large number of people felt that it was right that something should be done to settle the dispute. Some of them liked some of the ideas, and some did not. The islanders must be allowed to make up their own minds. The hon. Gentleman is rushing it a bit in trying to anticipate what they may eventually decide.

Mr. Peter Tapsell (Horncastle): Will my hon. Friend bear in mind that some of us who have interested ourselves in the future of the Falkland Islands over the years have considerable doubts about the tactical wisdom of placing the leasing point on the negotiating table? We therefore particularly welcome that part of his statement which said that no settlement would be pursued which did not have the support of the Falkland islanders.

Mr. Ridley: No offer has been made to the Argentine Government to negotiate on anything. This was a visit to consult the islanders about what they would like to see in any future negotiation or, in the case of a negative answer, if there were to be no future negotiation. There is no question about this being a negotiating offer on the table. This is something which the islanders will discuss among themselves in order to decide whether they wish it to be pursued.

Mr. Frank Hooley (Sheffield, Heeley): Is not the Government's argument that the interests of 1,800 Falkland islanders take precedence over the interests of 55 million people in the United Kingdom?

Mr. Ridley: There need be no conflict between the two, especially if a peaceful resolution of the dispute can be achieved.

Mr. Julian Amery (Brighton, Pavilion): Is my hon. Friend aware that his statement is profoundly disturbing? Is he also aware, certainly the Falkland islanders are, that for years—and here I speak from some experience—his Department has wanted to get rid of this commitment? Is he further aware that it is almost always a great mistake to get rid of real estate for nothing, that the Falkland Islands may have an important part to play in the future of the South Atlantic and that admitting that the interests of the inhabitants and their wishes must be paramount, there is also a considerable British interest in maintaining this commitment, which is probably much cheaper to maintain than it is to lose? Will my hon. Friend look back at the cost to us in terms of oil prices of the surrender of Aden and the Persian Gulf?

Mr. Ridley: I think my right hon. Friend knows me well enough to realise that I do not embrace schemes which are thrust upon me by my Department. The Government as a whole have taken the decision to take this initiative. It is of a political nature, and it is not the job of the Foreign Office to devise such an initiative. There is a great deal in what my right hon. Friend said about the need to watch the strategic and other interests in the South Atlantic. It is in order to ensure that these may be peacefully pursued, including the possibilities of oil around the Falklands, that there is a premium on trying to solve the dispute.

Mr. Donald Stewart (Western Isles): In order to allay the fears and doubts which his statement will have aroused among islanders, and in order to preserve the honour of the Government in the affair, will the Minister now advise the Argentine Government that the matter is closed unless and until the islanders wish to reopen it?

Mr. Ridley: I repeat that I was in the islands more recently that the right hon. Gentleman. It is not for him to say what the islanders do or do not want. I have asked them directly, and I do not need his services to anticipate what they may say.

Mr. Kenneth Warren (Hastings): I recognise that the Falkland Islands have severe current economic problems, but does my hon. Friend agree that the potential in terms of fisheries and offshore oil in the Falkland Islands is sufficient to sustain them economically in the not too distant future and that we should give the islanders every support that we can in their economic bargaining?

Mr. Ridley: My hon. Friend is right, but he will also know that it has not proved possible under the Governments of either party to exploit those resources, either of fish or oil, because of the dead hand of the dispute with Argentina. We are seeking to find a solution in order to make that possible.

Mr. Tom McNally (Stockport, South): Is the Minister aware that his Department's policy over many years has been the major cause of the uncertainty affecting the islands? Instead of making these humiliating excursions to the Argentine, would it not be better for the hon. Gentleman simply to say that whatever the Government, and whatever the majority, there will never be a majority in this House to give this historically separate people and separate islands to the Argentine?

Mr. Ridley: The hon. Gentleman speaks as if he knows more about the position than the Foreign Office and the islanders; he seems to speak for the whole House. He may find that he is sometimes wrong.

Viscount Cranborne (Dorset, South): Is my hon. Friend aware that his statement today has caused grave disquiet throughout his own supporters and that merely by entertaining the possibility of the surrender of sovereignty he is encouraging the islanders to think that they do not enjoy the support that they deserve from their home country? Is he also aware that his attitude reminds me of the attitude of the Church of England over the old Prayer Book—

Mr. Deputy Speaker: Order.

Mr. Ridley: I was happy to be able to assure the islanders that they had our support, whatever course they chose to take. Of course, whether the position remains as it is at present or whether there is a lease back, the Government are obligated to defend their territories all round the world.

Mr. Douglas Jay (Battersea, North): It is clear that the islanders, whatever else they may think, have no wish for a change of sovereignty. Why cannot the Foreign Office leave the matter alone?

Mr. Ridley: The right hon. Gentleman should have accompanied me on my visit; it would have been very pleasant. He may then have heard the views of the islanders, a large number of whom believe that it would be to their advantage to settle the dispute. He must listen to the views in the islands instead of preaching what he has always believed to be the case.

Several Hon. Members rose—

Mr. Deputy Speaker: Order. I must protect the business on the Order Paper. I propose to take three more questions from either side of the House.

Mr. Robin Maxwell-Hyslop (Tiverton): Did my hon. Friend discuss with the islanders the question of their right of access to the United Kingdom in any proposed change of the nationality laws, or did he tell them that a Home Office Minister would be visiting the Falkland Islands to do so? In other words, is it only to the House of Commons that my hon. Member will not answer questions about that, or will a Home Office Minister do so?

What is the position concerning Falkland Islands trade with Southern Chile? There was some experimental trade in lamb. What opportunities are there for further economic links between Southern Chile and the Falkland Islands rather than that the Falkland Islands should be totally reliant on Argentina?

Mr. Ridley: The islanders certainly discussed the question of nationality with me, and I said that I would discuss the matter with my right hon. Friend the Home Secretary when I returned home. I am sure that my right hon. Friend will discuss the matter with me at some stage.

The question of trade with Chile is open. There is no reason why the islanders should not trade with Chile, or with any other country. There has been one delivery of sheep to Chile, and we hope that there will be further trade between the two countries.

Mr. James Johnson (Kingston upon Hull, West): The House will welcome, and has welcomed, the Minister's unequivocal statement that the islanders will be the arbiters and sole judges of their destiny, but what is he doing to ameliorate their conditions? The islands are 10,000 miles away with a diminishing population, and young people are leaving them. Argentina will not go away, so the Government's duty is to ameliorate conditions between the islands and the mainland. What are the Government doing about fishing ventures, or any other commercial exploitations?

Mr. Ridley: I am taking an initiative to see, with the islanders, whether there is a way of solving the dispute. That is the way to unlock the economic potential that the islanders so badly need.

Mr. Matthew Parris (Derbyshire, West): Will my hon. Friend explain why the continuing dispute with Argentina precludes help from the United Kingdom Government to the islanders in developing their territory?

Mr. Ridley: The possibility of declaring a 200-mile zone round the islands is remote without the agreement of the Argentine, because of the difficulty of enforcing the licensing of fishing or oil exploration. Successive Governments found that that was not possible in the absence of an agreement. There is also considerable difficulty relating to investment and the extension of credit to the islands because of the fear of investors that the dispute may frustrate their investment.

Mr. John Home Robertson (Berwick and East Lothian): Will the Minister tell the House more about the leasing proposals? Is it his idea to sell the freehold to Argentina and to lease it back as part of the Government's attempt to reduce the public sector borrowing requirement?

Mr. Ridley: The details of any leaseback arrangement would first have to be considered by the islanders, and then it would be the subject of negotiation with the Argentine and then the subject of endorsement by the islanders and this House. It is impossible to go into detail with any accuracy, but it is not envisaged that any money would change hands, either in the transfer or in the lease.

Mr. William Shelton (Streatham): I congratulate my hon. Friend on taking the views of the islanders, which is right and proper. Will he confirm that should those views be for a maintenance of the status quo he will accept that? Will he also say whether he has contingency plans to help the islanders, despite the lack of resolution of the problem?

Mr. Ridley: We shall have to wait for the answer. That is a hypothetical question, and we must consider the matter when we hear from the islanders.

Mr. David Lambie (Central Ayrshire): As one of the few Members to have visited the Falkland Islands, may I ask the Minister whether he is aware of the deeply felt suspicion of the islanders of previous British Governments and British politicians, especially those representing the Foreign Office? Is he further aware that there was no need for today's statement, which will further heighten those suspicions? Is this a further example of the Government reneging on previous promises that were given to those people?

Mr. Ridley: As one of the few hon. Members to have visited the Falkland Islands—I have visited them twice—I beg to differ with the hon. Gentleman. My welcome was friendly, and the islanders were kind and listened to me with great attention. They were grateful for the frank discussions that we had.

Mr. Shore: The Minister was asked a few moments ago whether, if the islanders were to opt for the status quo, that would then be the Government's view on the matter and they would sustain it. He did not give a clear reply to that. If the Government are to honour their commitment that the views and wishes of the Falkland Islands are to be paramount, which is the word which has been used hitherto, he must assure the House and the Falkland islanders that that principle of paramountcy of their wishes about their future will be sustained by the British Government.

Mr. Ridley: I have said that anything that was proposed would have to be endorsed by the islanders. There is no need to repeat that. However, I cannot answer a hypothetical question about what might happen in certain circumstances just as I am sure that the right hon. Gentleman would not be prepared to say that, if the islanders endorsed a solution, he could make his whole party vote for it.

Mr. Farr: On a point of order, Mr. Deputy Speaker. Is it possible to give notice after a ministerial statement that one would wish to raise a matter on the Adjournment? If it is possible, I should like so to do because of the intense dissatisfaction I feel about what the Minister said.

MAP OF THE SOUTH ATLANTIC SHOWING THE FALKLAND ISLANDS AND THE FALKLAND ISLANDS DEPENDENCIES.

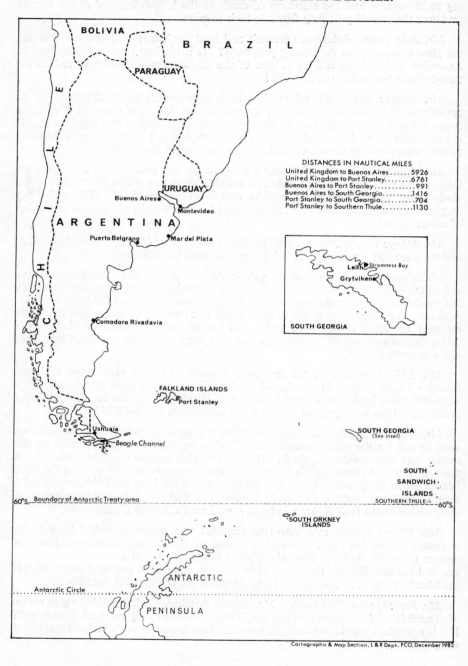

DISTANCES IN NAUTICAL MILES
United Kingdom to Buenos Aires......5926
United Kingdom to Port Stanley.......6761
Buenos Aires to Port Stanley...........991
Buenos Aires to South Georgia........1416
Port Stanley to South Georgia.........704
Port Stanley to Southern Thule........1130

Cartographic & Map Section, L & R Dept., FCO, December 1982

Printed in England by Her Majesty's Stationery Office

3145006   Dd 0203421   C160   1/83

ISBN   0   10   187870   2